CURATING ORAL HISTORIES

To the memory
of
Willa Klug Baum, 1926–2006

CURATING ORAL HISTORIES

From Interview to Archive

Nancy MacKay

Left Coast
Press Inc.
Walnut Creek, California

Left Coast Press Inc.

LEFT COAST PRESS, INC.
1630 North Main Street, #400
Walnut Creek, CA 94596
http://www.LCoastPress.com

Library of Congress Cataloging-in-Publication Data

MacKay, Nancy, 1945-
    Curating oral histories : from interview to archive / Nancy MacKay.
        p. cm.
    Includes bibliographical references and index.
    ISBN-13: 978-1-59874-057-8 (alk. paper)
    ISBN-10: 1-59874-057-1 (alk. paper)
    ISBN-13: 978-1-59874-058-5 (pbk. : alk. paper)
    ISBN-10: 1-59874-058-X (pbk. : alk. paper) 1. Libraries--Special
collections--Oral history. 2. Sound archives. 3. Oral history. I.
Title.
    Z688.O52M33 2007
    025.2'882--dc22

2006026624

07 08 09 10 11 5 4 3 2

Editorial Production: Last Word Editorial Services
Typesetting: ibid, northwest

Printed in the United States of America

♾™ The paper used in this publication meets the minimum requirements of American National Standard for Information Sciences—Permanence of Paper for Printed Library Materials, ANSI/NISO Z39.48–1992.

CONTENTS

PREFACE

The seed for this book was planted at the 2003 Oral History Association conference where I joined three other librarians and archivists on a panel to discuss oral histories in libraries. Though our session was scheduled early on a Saturday morning, our meeting room was packed. The audience was obviously eager to glean wisdom from our experience, and many stayed afterward to ask questions. It was clear that interest in oral histories in libraries and archives was high, and that there were more questions than answers in the air.

I, too, had more questions than answers.

The year before the conference I was asked to set up and manage a small oral history program at Mills College in Oakland, California, where I work as a librarian. As a cataloger for twenty-two years and a practicing oral historian for about sixteen, I'm familiar with the practices of each field, but when it came to bridging the gap between conducting oral histories and caring for them, I was stumped.

I faced the challenges of any new oral history program: space, equipment, record keeping, and cataloging. I found plenty of information on interview methods and oral history theory, but was hard put for guidance on what happens after the interview: processing, cataloging, rights management, preservation, and access. I muddled through that first year, creating forms and procedures and generally reinventing the wheel, but the experience motivated me to learn more about the state of oral histories in the repositories which become their permanent home.

I wanted to collect some data to back up my hunches, so in the spring of 2004 I conducted a survey[1] on oral histories in libraries and archives. I asked about the size and scope of oral history collections, about cataloging, about formats. I asked about the organizational structure of the repository—the kind of institution and the professional background of staff members. I asked about special problems associated with oral histories, and if they were often neglected (my suspicion) in the library or archive. I was eager to hear about the impact of technology, and how participants handled the preservation of deteriorating recording media. Finally I asked about dreams for the future.

Sixty-three responses came in from oral history repositories around the world—national libraries, universities, public libraries, corporate archives, community projects, and individuals. The results confirmed my suspicion that the majority of professionals charged with caring for oral histories are doing so in the dark.

I followed this survey with case studies of seven oral history programs that are particularly successful in meeting the challenges of the 21st century, that is, using technology wisely, participating in collaborative ventures, using the Internet for universal access, and making best use of human resources. Each program has a different organizational structure and set of goals, but they all successfully accomplish what they set out to do. Their comments and wisdom anchor the ideas in this book to real life experience.

All my investigations point to the information gap between the creators of oral histories and those who care for them. The need for standards, best practices, and a spirit of collaboration is essential as we move into the 21st century, to ensure that the work of oral historians is preserved as part of our cultural heritage. *Curating Oral Histories* is a step toward this goal.

ACKNOWLEDGMENTS

If this book realizes any success, it is because of the generosity of archivists, community historians, oral historians, and technical experts around the world whose experience I have compiled and built upon. This is truly a multidisciplinary and collaborative work.

The book is built around the responses to my 2004 survey. Archivists and curators took the time to analyze their collections, share their experience, and ask the hard questions. My first thank-you goes to all of you.

Seven oral history program managers participated actively in my research, taking the time to complete an extensive questionnaire, answer my detailed follow-up questions, and extend hospitality when I visited. I thank you from the bottom of my heart: Geoff Froh and Tom Ikeda at Denshō; Joan Craig at the Veterans Oral History Project, Morse Institute Library; Susan Becker at the Maria Rogers Oral History Program; Stephanie George and Art Hansen at the Center for Oral and Public History; Robyn Russell at the UAF Oral History Program; Troy Reeves at the Idaho Oral History Center; and Mary Ruth Thurmond and Richard Verrone at the Oral History Project, Vietnam Archive.

Others read sections of the manuscript with an expert eye, and offered suggestions based on a lifetime of experience or cutting-edge knowledge of current practice, as well as help with terminology in a field where the vocabulary is still finding its ground. Deepest thanks to Vivian Pisano, John Neuenschwander, Debbie Hansen, Geoff Froh, and Jennifer Myronuk. Errors, discrepancies, and shifts in accepted practice are bound to come up in a field as quickly evolving as this. If there are errors or lapses in judgment in how to present this material, they are entirely my own.

To Debbie Hansen, Joan Craig, and Barb Sommer, my deepest appreciation for taking time out of your professional lives to read the entire manuscript. Each of you brought an expert eye from a different perspective, and you will see the results of your wisdom in this final draft.

Thank you, Mitch Allen, for believing in me from the beginning and all the way through, even when I didn't believe in myself, and for keeping things light in those dark moments. Thank you, Joe Ryshpan, for your sharp editorial eye. Thank you, Robyn Russell, for planting the idea for this project in my head.

I am indebted to Willa Baum, who recognized the importance of a strong relationship between oral historians and libraries back in the 1970s. Her work laid the foundation for all of mine. Willa's passing, just as I was putting the final touches on this manuscript, paralyzed me temporarily, since so much of her spirit lives in these pages. Willa saw the early drafts of this book, but unfortunately not the finished work. I also knew Willa on a personal level, since our families were joined by marriage, and my fond memories include babysitting her grandchildren (who were my niece and nephews), family gatherings, and Monday night dinners around Willa's large oak table in Berkeley. Mentor, friend, and family member, in my mind Willa will always be the grandmother of oral history.

Most of all, thanks to my family, who put up with playing second fiddle during this year of writing. Christiaan, you gave me the writing bug, and now I'm stuck with it. Michael, you set me on the course for seeking the Truth, and you never let me stray. Jonathan, your roots provide the anchor so I can spread my wings. Your loving presence in my life underpins all my creative work, and casts the light that guides the way.

Thank you, Taos, New Mexico, where most of the writing was done. I am grateful for the fresh mountain air that kept my mind clear, and the desert expanses that made space for my creative juices. The summer I spent in Taos working on this book is one of the most productive and creative periods of my life. I hope the spirit of the mountains shines through.

INTRODUCTION

You are a librarian in a small public library. A local organization conducted a community oral history project and donated 1,200 interview tapes to your library. Most tapes are labeled and there is an inventory, but you must find a way to catalog, copy, shelve, and make them available to the public. Soon!

You are the new office manager for a large urban church. You come across a box labeled "Oral history interviews—civil rights workers—1964–1969." Many tapes are unlabeled, the physical condition is uncertain, yet they seem like valuable documents. What next?

You are a historian and have just received a grant to set up an archive—physical and digital—on the American immigrant experience, drawing on oral history projects around the country. You have the money and the subject expertise, but where can you turn for guidance on the nuts and bolts for assembling and managing this collection?

Sound familiar? Then welcome to the world of curating oral histories. If you find yourself in a situation like any of these, you are like great numbers of professionals, myself included, who must make decisions about the administration, cataloging, preservation, and access for oral histories, and have no place to turn for guidance.

Who are we—those of us charged with the care of oral histories? Judging by the responses to my 2004 survey,[1] we are an enormously diverse group. Our job titles range from historian to librarian to archivist to park ranger to community relations director. Some of us are volunteers who manage a single community project; others of us are administrators responsible for a large archive of which oral histories are just a tiny part.

Our educational background? Though most of us have advanced training in history, archives, or library science, others are doing this work because of interest or expertise in the topic at hand. Increasingly, full- and part-time technical experts appear on the staff roster.

Though our backgrounds and work situations are diverse, our unanswered questions are amazingly similar. These concerns were expressed in almost every survey:

- Need better communication among curators, oral historians, and other team members;
- Need standards and best practices for all phases of collection management;
- Need guidance on technology;
- Need creative ways to meet expenses in an era of shrinking funds.

Dreams for the future? Respondents unanimously mentioned the possibilities of digital technologies and the World Wide Web for improved preservation and access.

We are passionate about our work—I know because my survey shows that, for the most part, we are overworked and underpaid. One way or another, most of us have found creative ways to make the best of limited resources. And, though we'd rather not admit it, we very likely have a shelf or a whole closet—as far out of sight as possible—where our unprocessed oral histories sit, waiting for answers to our many questions.

HOW THIS BOOK IS ORGANIZED

This book will introduce you to the tasks required in taking an oral history from the interview to archive. It outlines a number of technical concepts as they apply to oral histories—each of which could be a book in itself. I do not attempt to provide a one-stop shop for curating oral histories, but rather to make you aware of the right questions to ask, and to offer guidelines for planning for your own situation.

The body of the text is organized loosely around the tasks that define an archivist's work: acquisition, description, rights management, preservation, and access.

Appendix B has worksheets and sample forms that can be used as is or be adapted to your own situation.

The Glossary (Appendix C) is a compendium of terms from the many disciplines that inform oral history.

The Resources section (Appendix D) points you to *recent* print references, or to websites that are frequently updated.

Appendix E is a list of organizations that sponsor publications, conferences, online discussion groups, and tutorials. This kind of networking is essential for keeping up with a field as rapidly evolving as ours, and how I got much of the information for this book.

The accompanying website, http://www.nancymackay.net/curating, provides direct links to the online resources mentioned here, details of my research, and other supporting materials.

TERMINOLOGY

When a work draws on many disciplines, understanding the terms and concepts is the foundation for communication. Terminology is an important part of this book. The Glossary brings together terms from law, library science, archives, oral history, preservation, recording technology, and information technology. Terms defined in the glossary are indicated in **bold** when first used in a chapter, if the meaning is not clear from the context.

Some important terms and concepts, though, cannot be so easily defined. Either the concept itself is fuzzy or the popular use of the term differs from the technical definition. Here are some terms I've taken liberties with:

The job of a *curator* is generally more comprehensive than that of an *archivist* or *project manager*; but duties overlap depending on the needs of the project or institution. I use these terms somewhat interchangeably, opting for the term that fits best within the particular context.

A *repository* and an *archive* are similar, though repository refers to a physical site for storing documents—library, archive, or off-site storage facility—and archive refers to the materials being stored and the concept of archiving, as well as the physical site. I use the term repository to refer specifically to a physical site, and archive when the concept is more general.

A *project* has a specific goal and end date; a *program* is more permanent, and usually connected to an institution. Though the terms are distinct, their roles in the curating process overlap. I've often taken the shortcut of using the term *project* when I mean either.

I've also taken the liberty of using *archive* and *project* interchangeably when I discuss concepts that could apply to either.

I've borrowed the term *rights management* from the information technology world, as an umbrella term to describe all the legal steps involved in creating, donating, and using oral histories. When I want to be more specific, I use *legal papers*.

I make a distinction between *interview* and *oral history*. An interview is a recorded question and answer session completed in a single sitting—a component of a completed oral history. An oral history is a "package" which I call the intellectual unit: the interview or series of interviews supplemented with commentary, photos, timelines, clippings, and other materials the oral historian includes to provide context.

Medium or *media* refer to the physical devices that carry the spoken words of the interview—audiocassettes, CDs, etc. *Recording media* are the devices that capture the sound. *Storage media* are the devices that store the sound in the archive. *Preservation media* are the devices especially designed for long-term preservation. Though the official umbrella term for these media is *data carrier*, I have opted for the more common term, *recording media,* to speak of these physical carriers as a group.

My solution to the gender equity dilemma is to use the male pronoun for the narrator and the female pronoun for the oral historian/archivist/curator/interviewer.

GETTING STARTED

The best way to get started is to complete the *Self-Study* on the following page, and to read the guidelines that follow. This will help you assess your own situation and determine the best way to use this book.

SELF-STUDY

ORGANIZATION

1. Type. What is the purpose of your organization? How are the archive and the oral history project related? Does the archive collect materials other than oral histories?

2. Structure. Is the archive part of a larger organization? What is that relationship? What are your responsibilities? What are the benefits? Is the archive organized around formats, such as a sound archive; or topics, such as a historical society?

RESOURCES

1. Human. List staff members: their skills, their duties, and how much time they devote to oral histories. Include permanent staff, student workers, volunteers, consultants, and vendors.

2. Technical. List technology needs for computer hardware and software, recording and transcribing equipment, archiving, preservation, and access. Then list the available technology resources, including skills of staff members.

3. Financial. List funding sources and projected expenses. Is funding ongoing, intermittent, or one-time-only? Do current funds meet the needs of the organization? What are opportunities for increasing funds? For doing more with less? For sharing expenses in a collaborative venture?

4. Physical. List your needs for staff work space, temporary and permanent storage for completed oral histories, reading and listening space for users. Is it secure? Is it environmentally friendly for long-term storage? What are the opportunities for sharing space?

ORAL HISTORY COLLECTION

1. Legal papers. Are the legal papers for each oral history sufficient for the current requirements of your archive? How do you keep track of them? Does your collection include **orphaned** oral histories? If so, determine what can be done resolve the outstanding legal problems.

2. Acquisition. How are oral histories acquired? How many new oral histories are added each year? Are they added in batches or in a regular flow?

3. Inventory. How many *physical items* in the collection? List (estimate, if the collection is large) each type of physical material (tape, disc, transcript, etc.) and the number of items within each category.

4. Extent. How many *oral histories* in the collection?

5. Recording media. List all the *kinds* of recording media in the collection—audiocassette, reel-to-reel, videocassette, CD, DVD, etc.

6. Transcript. Are oral histories transcribed? If not, do you intend to have them transcribed?

7. Cataloging. Are oral histories cataloged? If so, does the cataloging meet current standards? Where do catalog records live? What cataloging resources are available to you?

8. Backlog. Are there oral histories waiting to be processed, transcribed, or catalogued? How many, and what needs to be done? Does the backlog increase over time?

INTERPRETING YOUR ANSWERS

ORGANIZATION

1. Type. The institutional structure of the organization will, to a large degree, determine the standards you follow, the staff resources, the technology available, and the institutional goals. Whether your institution is a library, historical society, or sound archive; large or small; rich or poor; private or public, this is the first question to ask.

It is also important to determine the relationship between the oral history project and the archive. If they are the same entity, then communication channels are probably well established. If they are different entities, make sure to get an agreement in writing of who does what, so that each party understands the work of the others.

2. Structure. If your archive is part of a large organization, such as a university or government agency, you probably have both benefits from and responsibilities to that organization. Be clear about what these are, and understand the chain of command. On the other hand, your archive may be part of a very small organization, or even be a one-person operation. If this is the case, then you have a lot of flexibility and control over the materials, but fewer resources to draw on for big-ticket items, such as cataloging and preservation. Whatever the situation, consider the benefits and drawbacks, and how you can maximize the available resources to meet the needs of your oral history collection.

RESOURCES

The resources at hand will factor into all your planning and decisions. For example, if technical expertise and equipment are available from a parent organization, you don't need to budget for them. If you can meet your staff needs with energetic volunteers, you may need a manager to coordinate their efforts. The curator's job is to realistically assess the needs of the archive and be creative with available resources to accomplish the project's goals.

1. Human. Depending on the nature of the project, you may need an archivist/curator, project manager, interviewers, subject experts, catalogers, transcribers, technical experts, and preservationists. People resources are the beginning and the end of any endeavor—all that really matters in the end. Whether they are permanent employees, students, consultants, or volunteers—praise them, inspire them, pamper them, and mine them for their skills and their contacts in the study community.

2. Technical. Technology needs are complicated and expensive, but essential in a modern archive. In this rapidly evolving arena, it is necessary to purchase and maintain recording equipment and media, and computer hardware and software on a regular basis. Be aware that most of what you learn, as well as the equipment you purchase, will become obsolete in a short time. This is a fact of life, and don't feel bad if you can't keep up with it. None of us can.

3. Financial. Since archives are dedicated to preserving collections for the long run, their safety depends on a stable repository with permanent funding. Developing and maintaining an oral history collection is expensive, so be realistic about financial limitations, and creative about seeking funds. Most expenses are for people and technology, and these can often be offset through creative partnerships, trading goods for services, or volunteer help.

4. Physical. The physical environment is an easily overlooked, but essential, ingredient to a successful archive. An archive needs three kinds of physical space. First, it needs office space—desks and computers for staff, and workspace for processing oral histories. Second, it needs secure and environmentally friendly storage space for the oral histories themselves. Third, it needs a reading/listening room for users, with proper playback equipment. (See Chapter 2: Archives Administration.)

ORAL HISTORY COLLECTION

1. Legal Papers. This question is the very first one to ask, since no archive should accept an oral history without the proper legal papers specifying physical and intellectual ownership, restrictions if any, and access rights. (See Chapter 3: Legal & Ethical Issues.)

2. Acquisition. Oral histories come to an archive in a variety of ways, and each scenario presents a different approach:

- The archive and the oral history project are the same institution, so the workflow from interview to archive is relatively seamless.

- The archive and the oral history project are different, but they have established a relationship before the interviewing begins.

- A donor offers an oral history collection after the interviewing is complete—sometimes many years after.

- The archive discovers oral histories in its physical possession, but has not accessioned them, inventoried them, or processed them.

In each case, the curator should determine the size, physical condition, and content of the collection, and determine an accessioning and processing plan based on the answers. (See Chapter 2: Archives Administration.)

3. Inventory. An inventory is concerned with the physical units. Counting physical items will help determine processing and storage needs. Each physical item—tape, transcript, user copy, master copy, etc.—must be handled many times as it is accessioned, labeled, inventoried, evaluated, and eventually shelved.

Terminology Note: Physical Unit vs. Intellectual Unit

The *physical unit* and the *intellectual unit* relate to each other in important ways regarding cataloging, storage, and preservation. For example, an **oral history (intellectual unit)** needs to be catalogued, processed, and preserved as a unit. Each oral history consists of **physical units**: discs, tapes, transcripts, and data files in any number of versions or copies, which need to be reproduced, reformatted, and preserved.

It is important to distinguish between the physical and the intellectual units, and to keep track of the relationships among the parts.

---

4. Extent. The extent is concerned with the intellectual units. Each oral history may be catalogued, transcribed, summarized, or indexed. Each of these analytical tasks requires skilled staff time and expertise.

5. Recording media. A list of the recording media will help assess preservation needs. Each type of media has special needs regarding physical care, preservation, cataloging, and storage. The more formats, the more management. Here it will suffice just to list the media and approximate the numbers.

6. Transcripts. As curator, you are concerned about transcripts for two reasons. The first is preservation: If oral histories are transcribed, the content is secure, even if the recording media are deteriorating. The second is resource allocation: Transcription is a labor-intensive and expensive task which requires skilled workers and specific instructions from the curator. (See Chapter 5: Transcribing.)

7. Cataloging. Cataloging systems range from very simple to very complex, but the purpose is always to record data consistently and accurately, so users can find the information they need. Cataloging by trained librarians is usually the best solution, so if your project is connected to a library, make friends with the catalogers there. If not, create your own cataloging system on a database, spreadsheet, or on paper. The important thing is to get the information recorded as soon after its creation as possible. (See Chapter 6: Cataloging.)

8. Backlog. A backlog in cataloging, processing, or preservation is an unfortunate fact of life in most archives. If you have a serious backlog, do an item-by-item assessment to determine areas that need immediate attention—for media deterioration, missing information, or high-demand content. Based on these results, set priorities for tasks most in need of attention. Hopefully, you can work through the backlog gradually. If the backlog grows over time, consider **outsourcing** or streamlining tasks, or adding new staff.

CHAPTER 1

SETTING THE STAGE

We often create artificial distinctions between those who collect, those who research and report on, and those who preserve the record. When these are not the same person, their interests become compartmentalized, and there are too few opportunities to transfer understanding from recording session to future listeners and viewers of the record. . . . [T]he curator of collections must serve the multiple and diverse interests of narrators, donors, and users.

—William Schneider

William Schneider's words resonated as I read the responses to my survey. Over and over curators described their frustration in trying to process documents so far removed from the oral historian and her intentions—interviews without labels, summaries, or transcripts, and legal consent forms that were missing or insufficient. The consequences of this disconnect between the creator and the curator bode ill for the very historical record we seek to enrich.

When I started thinking about this book I was dismayed there was no term to aptly describe my topic. I had to search all the way back to 1978, to an essay by Willa Baum[1] calling for a stronger relationship between oral historians and librarians. She discussed curating as an essential library function and one of the "four Cs" in oral history.[2]

In rereading her essay, I was shocked that the questions Baum raised in the late 1970s are the very questions that plague us today: Who owns the tape? Who can grant permission to reproduce it? How should it be catalogued? Must the cataloger listen to the entire interview to determine the subject headings? Is the library liable if something defamatory is said in the interview?[3] Indeed, methodol-

ogy for curating oral histories sadly lags behind the excellent methodology for collecting them.

CURATING, AN OVERVIEW

Curation refers to the long-term care and management of historical documents, in order to ensure maximum access for the present and the future. It includes the archival process but goes beyond it. Here are some principles of curation as they apply to oral history.

Infrastructure

Oral histories need a physical home and, increasingly, a virtual home. They need an administrator who understands the organizational structure of the holding institution, the physical and intellectual characteristics of oral histories, the technical requirements of preserving them, and the user audience. Since oral histories have special needs and often get buried in the backlog, the curator must advocate on their behalf to funding agencies and policy makers.

Record Keeping

Meticulous record keeping is essential to a well-managed archive. Records include a complete and accurate inventory of holdings; a **management system** to track processing, cataloging, restrictions, legal papers, and items missing; and a file for proper names and dates, verified and spelled consistently.

Rights Management

Rights management for oral histories includes tracking restrictions, intellectual property rights, and permission to use. These complex issues are specific to each archive, and should be reviewed by administrators and legal experts within the institution.

Cataloging

The primary purpose of cataloging is to direct users to the information they seek, as quickly and precisely as possible. Cataloging can also track administrative information, and provide an inventory. There are several models for cataloging oral histories but currently no standards.

Preservation

The goal of any archive is to preserve its collections into the indefinite future. As we move from an analog to a digital environment, there is much confusion about best preservation practices for oral histories, but currently no standards.

Access

A corollary to preservation is access: archives have a mission to make their holdings available to users. Traditionally, that meant making a transcript and/or recording available in a repository. But modern archival practice calls for a more proactive approach to access, including educational outreach, publications, displays, and online exhibitions.

ORAL HISTORY, AN OVERVIEW

The task and theme of oral history—an art dealing with the individual in social and historical context—is to explore this distance and this bond [between "history" and personal experience], to search out the memories in the private, enclosed space of houses and kitchens and—without violating that space, without cracking the uniqueness of each spore with an arrogant need to scrutinize, to know, to classify—to connect them with "history"—and in turn force history to listen to them.

—Alessandro Portelli[4]

Alessandro Portelli captures the essence of oral history so beautifully. More simply defined, oral history is a method of documenting recent history through the words of those who lived it. Practitioners have refined the definition to include these characteristics to distinguish oral history from journalism, ethnography, or other kinds of interviewing.

Question and Answer Format

Narratives are collected in an interview format with the interviewer asking questions and the **narrator** responding.

Respect for the Narrator

An oral history is considered a collaborative work, with the narrator the primary creator. If there is a conflict, the narrator's wishes should prevail. Generally the interviewer controls the *structure* of the interview, and the narrator controls its *content*.

Highest Quality Recording

Since archived interviews will be listened to over and over into the future, interviewers should make recording quality a high priority. Interviewers should use the best recording equipment available to them, and develop the skill to use it proficiently.

Subject Expertise

Interviewers should develop expertise in the subject of the interview and prepare by choosing topics and questions carefully.

Archiving

The completed oral history should be catalogued, copied to preservation media, and deposited into an appropriate archive for permanent storage and access.

Professional Standards

Practitioners have an ethical responsibility to the narrator, to the institution they represent, and to the profession. Oral historians should follow the standards and guidelines issued by the Oral History Association and the American Historical Association.

Within these parameters, oral historians approach interviewing from various perspectives. At one end of the spectrum is the life history interview, which consists of a number of in-depth interviews documenting one person's life. At the other end is the topical interview, which consists of multiple interviews organized around a topic or event. These interview styles can be combined or adapted to suit the mission of the project at hand. Whatever the approach, it needs to be communicated to the curator, because it will affect decisions in record keeping, cataloging, and preservation.

THE REPOSITORY

The repository is the physical site where oral histories are kept. Libraries and archives are the most traditional repositories for oral histories, but historical societies, museums, schools, community centers, religious institutions, and corporations hold oral histories as well. A repository can be as simple as a closet or a file cabinet in the director's office, or as large and well-equipped as a presidential library. Each has a different organizational structure, set of goals, and resources. For most, caring for oral histories is only a small part of the mission. Yet curators from every repository must find a way to store, catalog, and preserve oral histories, all within the confines of their institutional mission and resources at hand.

The responses to my survey highlight this diversity: twenty-one came from academic institutions, thirteen from publicly funded historical societies, six from various national government archives (from the U.S., U.K., and Canada), and twenty-one from private and community projects. Two respondents have an online presence only.

WHAT'S SO HARD ABOUT CURATING ORAL HISTORIES?

Oral histories all too often end up in the back room of the repository, unprocessed and forgotten. The archivist discovers the tapes are unlabeled and puts the project aside; the cataloger is confounded by the formats, so she returns the cassette and transcripts to her problem shelf; the curator discovers the legal consent forms don't meet the requirements for the institution, so she throws in the hat as well. These are just some of the problems that keep oral histories on the margins in archives. Some of the problems are inherent to the nature of oral history and will be addressed throughout the book; others stem from poor communication between the creators and the curators of the materials. Here are some of the obstacles curators face.

Rights Management

This is a complex issue that everyone tends to shy away from, yet it is essential to a properly managed archive. Generally, rights management refers to the bundle of legal transactions associated with accessioning the oral history into the archive, honoring any restrictions attached to it, and managing its use. In real life, oral histories end up in the repository with legal papers missing, inadequate for current standards, or with complicated restrictions. The time and expertise required to remedy inadequate legal papers is enormous and expensive, and sometimes leads to dead ends. Curators must decide whether to allocate precious staff time to do this research. To further complicate things, curators now face new legal issues regarding the posting of interviews on the Internet. The result of these complexities, sadly but understandably, often keeps oral histories from public access.

Orphaned Documents

These are documents in an archive which cannot be made available to the public for some reason—the legal consent form is missing or inadequate; the document itself is too fragile to handle; or in the case of sound recordings, the media format is obsolete and can't be played. Oral histories are doubly vulnerable to orphan status because of their complicated legal status and because of the obsolescence factor of recording media. Orphaned documents pose a major dilemma for curators, who must weigh the enormous cost in staff resources to rectify the problems against the cost of allocating storage space for documents that can't be properly processed for public use.

Transcript or Recording—What Is the Primary Document?

This is an important intellectual question for historians, but for curators it is a practical one: "Should it be processed as a sound recording, a manuscript, or a book?" Early oral history practice favored the *transcript* as the primary archival document, and the recording was discarded. Current practice considers the *recording* the primary document. Most archival collections hold and continually process both transcripts and recordings, as well as a combination of the two. Since each format is

handled very differently in the archive, curators must develop procedures for cataloging and processing materials that ensure consistency for the collection, while at the same time comply with the standards of the institution.

Formats and Media

Analog or digital? Optical or magnetic? Tape or disc? Physical medium or **media independent**? And the list goes on, thoroughly confusing all of us. The multitude of formats and media which record and preserve oral histories each have special requirements for physical storage, preservation, cataloging, and playback. Curators must meet these needs for each item in the collection, and at the same time be prepared for their obsolescence as new technologies take their place.

In my discussions with curators from archives around the country, I learned that real-life situations are far from ideal, even when curators understand the special issues concerning oral histories. Because of these complexities and the skilled expertise it takes to remedy them, too many oral histories stay on the problem shelf.

The practice of *curating* oral histories lags behind the practice of *creating* them. Sometimes the complexities—diverse institutional practices, rapidly evolving technology, lack of standards, rights management, and confusion about oral history itself—seem overwhelming. Creators of oral histories must understand how curators work and what tools they need to preserve and provide access to oral histories. Curators need a baseline or standard from which to accomplish this.

WHEN TO CONSULT AN EXPERT

Most of the time, archives function well on their own. Curators develop policies and procedures that fit their mission and their resources. But every now and then, situations arise when serious damage can be done to a collection without the help of experts. These are some situations when it is important to get expert advice.

- Contact a *subject expert* if you suspect you have recorded interviews with significant content, but do not have a legal consent form, proper labels, or a collection summary.

- Contact a *legal expert* if you suspect that legal papers are missing or don't reflect the current needs of the archive.

- Contact a *preservation expert* before undertaking a large digitization project, if you have tapes that are more than fifteen years old, or if you have oral histories on earlier media formats (reel-to-reel tape or cylinders). Do not play tapes if you suspect they are damaged.

THE BOTTOM LINE

It's easy to get discouraged about creating a perfect home for oral histories, but in fact, no repository, even the biggest and best funded, has a perfectly cared-for oral history collection. The important thing is to manage the collection the best you can with the resources available. These guidelines help you accomplish much with little.

- Always make user copies of recordings and keep originals in a separate physical location.

- Never accept materials without the proper legal papers established by your organization.

- Be meticulous about labeling and keeping records.

- Plan carefully for large-scale projects, such as cataloging and preservation. Learn from the experience of others by including colleagues and consultants in your plans.

- If you are processing a large collection, begin by making a careful assessment; then set priorities. Make materials with the most important content or most endangered physical media your highest priority.

- Keep in mind the ultimate goals: preservation and access.

CHAPTER 2

ARCHIVES ADMINISTRATION

Most of us who curate oral histories do so for the love of it, and we are amply rewarded. Our vaults are filled with voices—voices telling stories and singing songs, voices sharing laughter and tears, voices telling everyday stories about home life and giving personal accounts of world events. The recorded voice is the most human of all artifacts, and we are entrusted with preserving the voices of the past for the benefit of generations to come.

The archives profession is old and well established. Without archives, much of the world's cultural and historical heritage would be lost. In contrast to libraries, archives collect one-of-a-kind unpublished documents such as diaries, letters, legal papers, and oral histories—the primary documents upon which scholarship is based. Traditionally, archives collected paper documents because most of history was recorded that way. Today, collections include all kinds of artifacts, from clay tablets to sound recordings to digital files, each with specific requirements for storage, preservation, and access.

Archival work is organized around five tasks: acquisition, description, **rights management,** preservation, and access. The first of these tasks, acquisition, is covered in this chapter; the remaining four tasks are covered elsewhere in the book. Since so much excellent work is available on managing archives, this chapter focuses on selected topics especially relevant to oral histories in the archive.[1]

❖

GETTING STARTED

Since repositories and archives vary so much, it's a good idea to begin by looking carefully at the needs and circumstances of your own project or institution. Take a moment to review your answers to the *Self-Study* at the beginning of the book, and to the comments which follow.

Figure 2.1. Terminology Note: Repository vs. Archive

A *repository* is a physical site where documents are kept. It can be as tiny as a file cabinet drawer or as large as a national library.

An *archive* suggests something broader. It refers not only to the physical location but also to the documents themselves, the associated tasks required for managing them, and the professional responsibilities of the archivist. Though many oral history collections are housed in small, informal repositories which might not qualify as archives in a formal sense, the principles described here can be applied to an archive of any size.

No archive for your oral history collection? Then your first decision is whether to set up an in-house archive or seek an existing one as a permanent home for your oral histories. Keep in mind the dual purposes of every archive—preservation and access—and how each of these goals could best be achieved for your own materials. An established archive (one existing in another institution) has the advantage of institutional stability and the resources to preserve and care for materials into the future, but may not give oral histories the special attention they deserve. On the other hand, an in-house archive (one you created specifically for the project) has the advantage of local control and immediate access to users, but may not have the necessary institutional stability. Establishing a permanent home that best fits your oral history collection is the best assurance for its long-term care.

SETTING UP AN ARCHIVE

If you decide to keep oral histories in-house, you will be faced with certain tasks and decisions upfront. Begin by exploring opportunities to share space, staff, and technical resources with a parent institution or community partner. Such partnerships benefit everyone, as long as both parties clearly understand their rights and responsibilities.

Include the following when planning for an archive:

Physical Space

OFFICE NEEDS. Include space for a desk and computer for the archivist, workspace for processing oral histories, phone, Internet connection, and postal address.

STORAGE SPACE. Create secure and environmentally friendly storage space for oral history recordings (originals and copies), transcripts, and recording equipment.

PUBLIC READING/LISTENING/VIEWING AREA. Include a comfortable reading/listening/viewing room with playback equipment for users. Often this space can be shared: a library reading room or a community center meeting room.

Budget

Archives are generally underfunded, and archivists spend much of their time justifying budget requests. The needs of oral histories are especially misunderstood. Be sure to consider funds for transcription, digitization, and copying recordings, as well as the traditional needs of an archive: staff, space, computer software and hardware, and supplies.

Staff

Staffing a small archive can be a big problem, and may be a reason for turning the collection over to a larger institution. No matter what the size, most archives work best if one staff member can oversee all the operations. Other duties can be distributed among students, volunteers, or contractors.

Figure 2.2. Tips for Successful Record Keeping

- Determine exactly what information you need to track and record only that. Do not track unnecessary information.

- Record information as close to the time you receive it as possible.

- Always record information consistently and accurately.

Record Keeping

Meticulous record keeping is essential to a well-managed archive. Use one of the record-keeping methods in Figure 2.3 to plan and set up your own system for tracking stages of the project. Be sure to include the following:

LABELS. Every physical item should be labeled with the name of the narrator, the interviewer, and interview date. Most archives assign an **accession number** to link related physical items (e.g., recording media to transcripts) to each other, and to electronic records.

STATUS LOG. Set up a system to track every event in the oral history's life, from the time it is accessioned, through each processing step, to use, and preservation events after it is in the archive. Use or adapt the *Processing Checklist* in Appendix B to help organize your work.

Figure 2.3. Three Methods for Keeping Records

Paper. Create a form for each interview with the essential information. This can be printed and stored in a binder, or saved electronically. *Low-tech.*

Spreadsheet. Create a row for each interview and a column for each item to be tracked. Information can be sorted, viewed, hidden, or color-coded in a few keystrokes, and later exported to a database or collection management system. *Medium-tech.*

Database. Create a record for each interview with fields for each item to be tracked. Though databases make it possible to manipulate data easily, they also require a certain amount of expertise to design and maintain. This solution is best for managing larger collections. *High-tech.*

CONTACT LISTS. Keep contact information for present and past narrators, interviewers, transcribers, volunteers, and consultants. It's surprising how often you need it.

RIGHTS MANAGEMENT. Keep track of all the legal papers pertaining to each oral history— **deed-of-gift agreement**, **restrictions**, and permission to use. (See sample forms in Appendix B.) Paper files are best for these records, since the original signed documents must be kept. Restrictions are especially troublesome to track, so develop a system that readily identifies the restricted item and under what circumstances restrictions are lifted, in both the record-keeping system and the physical item.

Recording Equipment

The purchase, inventory, and maintenance of recording equipment is a small but important duty that often falls into the curator's hands. This task is so simple it is often overlooked, but the obvious consequences of nonfunctional recorders in a field setting are disastrous. (See Chapter 4: Recording Technology.)

A new archive has one big advantage: It is not bound by the practices and traditions of an earlier age. In setting up a new archive, develop standards, policies, and procedures that meet your specific needs and that make use of 21st century technology.

ACQUIRING AN ORAL HISTORY COLLECTION

Oral history collections offered to archives vary enormously in size, age, content, and physical condition. The net value of a collection to a particular institution is dependent on these factors, as well as the resources required to process and store it. Make selections carefully, and avoid accepting materials you cannot process in a timely manner, that have restrictions on the content, or that lack proper legal papers. A written **collection policy**, such as the sample in Appendix B, will keep the archive's focus clear over time, and clarify the archive's mission for potential donors. *The right match between an oral history collection and an archive is the most important ingredient to success.*

Oral histories come to an archive from various sources, and each situation requires a different approach. These are the common scenarios:

- Archive and oral history project are the same entity. This scenario makes it easiest for all parties. A parent institution is funding both, so has a vested interest in its success; the workflow is seamless; and chances are good that all the staff members are in the same physical location and communicate frequently.

- Oral history project has established a relationship with the archive before the interviewing begins. This is the best scenario for oral history projects not already connected to a library or archive. If an archive is selected before interviewing begins, then procedures can be established for processing or turning over materials to the archive, and agreement about costs for processing can be made upfront.

- Donor offers oral histories after the interviewing is complete. This is a common situation, but can be a troublesome one. Before accepting a collection, be sure to evaluate it using the criteria in the next section, and determine whether the new collection is appropriate to the scope and the resources of your institution.

- Special cases. Curators are occasionally confronted with additional acquisitions situations which must be handled on a case-by-case basis. Perhaps the archive discovers oral histories in its physical possession, but has not accessioned them, inventoried them, or processed them; or the archive is required by the institution to accept a collection; or oral histories come along as part of a larger collection.

No matter how oral histories come into the archive, curators must weigh a number of factors before accepting and **accessioning** them. The *content* of the oral history collection is the most important criterion, but it is not the only one. If the recordings require preservation work, or if labeling and cataloging require a great deal of research, then the curator must weigh the value of the content against the resources required to process, preserve, and provide access to them.

EVALUATING AN ORAL HISTORY COLLECTION FOR ACQUISITION

Now that you are considering a new collection for the archive, you need to evaluate it for content, size, and condition. Use or adapt the *Collection Evaluation for Accession* worksheet in Appendix B. (If the collection is large or if you find unexpected problems, break it down into smaller groups and repeat the evaluation.) The results will provide a summary of the collection, and from there you can decide on the best way to process these materials and prioritize tasks.

Content

This deals with the *intellectual* content of the materials. How do they relate to each other or to the existing collection? Are there other relationships within the materials, such as a common narrator or a common topic? Is the content unique to the collection or to the world of knowledge? Does the collection provide a different perspective?

Legal Papers

An archive can accept materials only from their legal owner, and procedures for accepting new collections are usually well established in archives. However, an additional document is necessary for oral histories—the original consent forms signed by the narrator and the interviewer. Make sure a consent form accompanies each interview, and that it meets the archive's standards. Be sure to check if the consent form states any restrictions on the materials. (See Chapter 3: Legal and Ethical Issues.)

Inventory

Now turn your attention to the size of the collection. Begin with *physical units*—each transcript, tape, CD, photograph, etc., counts as a unit. List each media type—paper, tape, disc—and count each item. (Estimate, if the collection is large.) This is important since each physical medium has special requirements for playback, cataloging, storage, and preservation, and each physical item needs to be handled many times. The physical size of the collection is a major factor in determining staff, storage, and processing requirements.

Now consider the oral histories as *intellectual units*. How many interviews? How many oral histories? A large collection will impact resources for cataloging and description; a very small donation without a context might have limited value.

Are parts of the collection missing? Will these missing parts compromise the value of the collection, or can they be acquired later? Are interviews still being conducted? If so, is there a procedure for new interviews to come into the archive? These are administrative questions that will affect the workflow, cataloging, storage, and preservation.

Physical Condition

Make a visual assessment of the physical condition, format by format. Is paper from transcripts brittle? Are tapes deteriorating? Do you know how materials were stored in the past? The evaluation can be superficial at this early stage, but as you begin to process the collection you will need to carefully examine and evaluate each item.

Existing Documentation

Are all recording media labeled with names of interviewer and narrator, and date and place of interview? If materials are delivered electronically, are software and hardware specifications documented? Is there an accompanying summary or catalog record to describe the collection or individual items? Is current contact information for the narrator and interviewer available? Without information about the oral history, its value is compromised. The curator must decide whether to invest staff time in the research to get this information, to process the materials anyway (generally not recommended), or to discontinue processing. Some curators insist that this documentation accompany a new collection.

When you have completed the evaluation to your satisfaction, use the results to develop a plan for accessioning and processing the collection for the archive.

ACCESSIONING AND PROCESSING AN ORAL HISTORY

Before you begin, determine if the materials are arranged in a particular order, for example, by donor, chronology, or topic; or if oral histories arrive as part of a collection of other materials (see Figure 2.4). If so, it is important to keep the **original order** intact when you do the evaluation, and all the way through the processing. If not, you can separate the materials into categories that make it convenient to evaluate, e.g., by physical medium, by chronology, or by topic.

Every oral history accessioned into the archive must go through certain steps to

---

Figure 2.4. Archival Principle of Arrangement

Archival materials are meaningful because of their *context* (physical relationships among the materials) as well as their *content*. Here are some terms archivists use to describe these relationships:

Provenance refers to the owner, or the succession of owners, of the documents.

Original order, or *respect des fonds*, refers to the original organization of the records, established by their creator.

Arrangement refers to the process of organizing the materials once they are in the archive, with respect to provenance and original order.

Curators should be aware that if oral histories accompany a larger collection—for example, the papers of an author—the oral histories should probably remain with the original collection.

prepare it for permanent storage and public use. Practices vary in the exact steps and how they are accomplished, but the important thing is that processing be done consistently, in a timely fashion, and that all work be well documented. This meticulous record keeping is an unpopular job for some, and where oral history projects often falter. Use or adapt the *Processing Checklist* in Appendix B to guide you.

The first step is to set up a system for keeping records. No matter what record-keeping method you use, create a record for each interview, and log each step when it is accomplished. For each step, record the date it was completed and by whom. Make notes on problems and missing documents.

Here are the common steps for processing an oral history:

1. **Log incoming oral history.** When the oral history arrives in the archive, log it into your record-keeping system. Include the name of interviewer and narrator, date of interview, date received, and notes about any special circumstances. Assign an accession number that will follow it through its life in the archive.

2. **Check legal papers.** Review the legal consent form and make sure it is correctly signed and dated, and note that it is received. Make a copy and keep the original with your permanent files.

3. **Copy and store the original recording.** Copy the original recording and store it in a safe, environmentally friendly location, preferably physically separate from the archive. The copy, called the **preservation master**, will be used to make subsequent copies for transcribers, for public use, or for the narrator. Be sure to label every copy.

4. **Transcribe.** There can be several steps to transcribing: sending the recording to the transcriber, receiving the completed transcript, **audit-checking** the transcript,

sending the transcript to the narrator for review, and processing (formatting, binding, etc.) the final transcript. Be sure to record every transcribing step as it is completed. (See Chapter 5: Transcribing.)

5. **Catalog.** The level of cataloging and the home for catalog records depends on the project, the requirements of the archive, and the resources at hand. Record the date when the cataloging is complete. (See Chapter 6: Cataloging.)

6. **Deposit into the archive.** This final step completes the processing, as the oral history officially enters the public record and is available for use.

7. **Thank the interviewer and narrator.** Send a note to the interviewer and the narrator when the oral history is completely processed and in the archive. This courtesy is always appreciated and brings closure to the oral history experience for the narrator and the interviewer. Be sure to keep contact information for the narrator and interviewer in your permanent files.

DIGITAL ARCHIVES

As if we curators didn't have enough to be confused about, digital technology is forcing us to look at every aspect of our work differently, and to consider the new opportunities it offers. Capabilities for storing vast quantities of data, including multimedia; for transport-

---

Figure 2.5. Terminology Note: Digital Archive vs. World Wide Web

A digital archive is a tool for preservation and a website is a medium for display and access. Sometimes oral histories that appear on a website are stored in a digital archive, but many are not.

ing this data easily and inexpensively; and for aggregating this data into large shared archives based on subject, ownership, or any other criterion, are all being experimented with as I write. The standards and best practices for digital archives now being debated will include **file format** standards, **metadata** standards, data transfer, shared data, rights management, and security.

Curators of oral histories could enter this debate with the following questions: (1) What is the role of the transcript in a keyword-searchable environment? (2) What metadata standards will be used for tracking and describing this data? (3) How are rights management, especially restrictions, tracked in a digital archive? (4) What are the opportunities and the cautions for sharing digital collections, and for contributing to a larger archive? (5) How can small institutions, which hold most oral histories, benefit from this technology?

THE BOTTOM LINE

Managing oral histories in an archive is a detailed job that requires multiple skills, judg-

ment, physical workspace, an adequate ongoing budget, and adequate technical support. It is rare that all these factors come together, and archivists must be creative about doing the best they can with available resources. Keep in mind the dual goals of preservation and access into the long-term future, and direct all your resources toward achieving them.

- Be consistent and detailed in record keeping.
- Always make user copies of recordings and store the original recording separately.
- If you have important materials that have immediate preservation needs, make them the highest priority.
- Develop short-term and long-term goals that are attainable with the resources at hand.

Useful Forms in Appendix B

Acquisitions Guidelines
Accession Form for Oral History Collection
Sample Collection Policy
Collection Evaluation for Accession
Processing Checklist

CHAPTER 3

LEGAL AND ETHICAL ISSUES

Recordings in an archive are subject to the concerns of at least five different interest groups: the interviewee, the interviewer, the community, the archive that manages the collection, and future users. The collections curator sits in the middle. This is a challenge. It's hard to create a five-way win-win agreement.

—William Schneider

We curators must juggle the interests of various communities, ride the fine line between legal and ethical matters, and do it all on time and within budget. Fortunately, oral history is a satisfying and fulfilling activity and legal problems rarely arise, but we must understand our rights and responsibilities concerning ownership, **copyright**, and use, and must secure the proper legal papers to back them up.

Each oral history accepted into an archive must be accompanied by a legal agreement acknowledging the transaction and clarifying certain other conditions. Since interviewer-narrator relationships, the goals of oral history projects, and the institutions they represent are all unique, each institution must draft legal papers specific to its own requirements.

Legal issues, however, are only part of doing oral history, and arise in the rare case when something goes wrong. Behind the legal papers are people telling stories, people recording them, and people ensuring their preservation and access. The ethical responsibilities that define the relationships among these people and institutions are the cornerstone of oral history practice.

This chapter is devoted to the legal and ethical issues that may come up when doing oral history. The first section explains the ways oral histories may touch the law, and what curators should be aware of. The second section describes ethical issues, and offers guidelines for ethical practice for the interviewer, the oral history program, and the archive. Appendix B has sample forms for various legal transactions.

LEGAL CONSIDERATIONS

Without a legal release, the possessor of the tape or transcript of an oral history interview cannot legally utilize, loan, publish, or make it available to researchers without infringing upon the rights of the interviewee and possibly the interviewer. . . . The importance of this requirement cannot be emphasized enough. The minimal time and cost that may be required to secure a legally sound and appropriate agreement can never outrun the long-term value to the program or the individual oral historian.[1]

John Neuenschwander's strong words underscore what is even more important for the curator of an archive than for an individual oral historian: *There is no point in undertaking the expensive activities of copying, processing, cataloging, and preserving oral history materials until all the legal papers are in order.*

There are three instances where oral histories touch the law. The first is the relationship between the narrator and the interviewer, which is defined in a document usually called the **legal consent form**, and should be signed by everyone speaking on the recording. The second is the relationship between the donor of the oral history (usually the oral historian or oral history project) and the receiving institution, transacted through a **deed-of-gift** agreement. When the oral history project and the repository are one in the same, or when the interviewer has made prior arrangements with the repository, these documents are usually bundled into a single form that transfers ownership and rights directly to the archive. The direct transfer from the narrator to the archive is the preferred practice, when it is possible. Figure 3.2 shows these relationships in diagram form.

For example, if I am an oral historian and have made a prior agreement with an archive to donate my interviews, the narrator and I can sign an agreement drawn up by the archive itself transferring rights. On the other hand, if I am an oral historian without a clear intent to archive my interviews, I will have the narrator (and myself) sign a legal consent form which gives me the rights to use his words in my work, and to donate the interview to an archive at a later date. When I'm ready to donate the interview to the archive, I will sign a deed-of-gift agreement which states that I, as legal owner of the interview, donate the recording and the accompanying copyrights, to the archive.

The third relationship concerns the *use* of oral histories in an archive. A form or letter addressed to the researcher and signed by the archivist should stipulate the requirements for publication and other use, and how to cite the oral history. See Appendix B for sample letter.

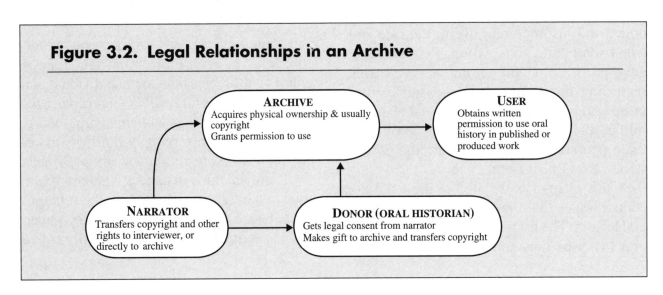

Figure 3.2. Legal Relationships in an Archive

All three of these relationships and the documents defining their legal status are essential to a well-managed archive. The deed-of-gift agreement and the permission-to-use agreements are legal declarations of which the archive is a party. The legal consent form between the narrator and the interviewer may be separate, but must accompany every oral history accessioned into the archive to show original proof of ownership.

Legal Consent Form

This agreement is signed by the parties whose voices appear on the recording, to "ensure the orderly and legally sound transfer of all rights sought by the program from the narrator and interviewer."[2] It should include the following:

TRANSFER OF OWNERSHIP. Usually this is accomplished through a deed-of-gift agreement.[3] The donor must show written proof of ownership in order for this transaction to take place. For oral histories, the owners are the speakers on the recording, unless otherwise specified. The speakers usually transfer ownership to the interviewer/project/archive by what oral historians call a legal consent form between the narrator and the interviewer/donor.

COPYRIGHT. Creators of a work automatically secure copyright at the point of creation. In the case of oral histories, this happens as soon as the recorder is turned off. Transferring copyright to the archive makes it convenient for future users to access and quote from these works without tracking down the original creators to get permission.

Most, but not all, archives keep control of copyright. The primary exception is the United States Government, which assigns all materials created under its auspices to the **public domain**. This means that researchers are free to use materials without seeking permission. However, even if a program chooses to place interviews in the public domain, the legal consent form must specifically stipulate this. *Relinquishing copyright is not the same as foregoing the legal consent form.*

VOLUNTARY PARTICIPATION. This clause acknowledges that the narrator is participating in the interview voluntarily.

CONTINUING RIGHTS OF THE INTERVIEWER AND NARRATOR. This clause exempts the narrator and interviewer from copyright restrictions and gives them the right to use their own words in future published or produced works. For example, "This gift does not preclude any use which we [names of narrator and interviewer] may make of our interview."

FUTURE USE. This clause states the intended use of the material. It should be as general as possible, e.g., ". . . may publish or otherwise use this work for such historical and scholarly purposes as it sees fit, including electronic distribution."

RESTRICTIONS. In addition to the clauses mentioned above that belong in every legal consent form, a narrator sometimes requests that certain restrictions apply to his interview once it is archived. Though it may make perfect sense from the historian's and the narrator's point of view, restrictions are difficult to manage in an archive. In fact, some archives will not accept interviews with restrictions. Decisions about managing restrictions must be made on a case-by-case basis, and only in exceptional cases. These are some common requests for restrictions:

- to seal the interview for a certain period of time, until the narrator's death or the death of someone mentioned in the interview;
- to remain anonymous; or
- to deny permission to publish on the Internet.

Oral Histories with No or Insufficient Legal Papers

Accessioning oral histories into the archive without the proper legal papers not only violates the standards of the oral history and the archives professions, but it may subject the archive and its parent institution to legal liability. That said, sometimes the content of the interviews may be so valuable that the curator must weigh the benefit of preserving them for the historical record against the consequences of keeping legally ambiguous materials in the archive.

If this is the case, curators should first make a diligent effort to contact the narrator or his heirs and secure a legal consent form. If this search is unsuccessful, curators should consult with their institution's legal counsel to decide if the materials can be made available in any form to the public. Since making legally ambiguous materials available for public use can subject the curator and the institution to liability, proceed with caution.

Permission to Use

PERMISSION TO QUOTE OR USE. Once the oral history has been legally accessioned into the archive, the next legal transaction is between the archive and the user: the permission to use the materials. Some archives have a standard form for this purpose; others simply write a letter giving permission.

FAIR USE.[4] The **fair use doctrine** makes an exception to the copyright restrictions for the sake of education and research. This is a fuzzy area of the law that is interpreted inconsistently in the scholarly community. It means that published and unpublished materials can be copied to a limited extent for noncommercial purposes, usually education. Oral histories fall under this doctrine in the way that any unpublished materials would.

Since there is almost no case law concerning oral histories, it is difficult to determine exactly how an infringement of copyright, fair use, or permission to use would be interpreted by the courts.[5] With this legal frontier before us, most curators err on the conservative side.

ETHICAL CONSIDERATIONS

In conducting and using oral history there are two principal ethical concerns. One is a concern for the interview process—methodology. The second is a concern for the person—the rights, privacy and dignity of the interviewee. The interviewer must always weigh the concern for professional research methodology against concern for the person being interviewed. The ethical concern for the person being interviewed should always outweigh concern for the interview process.[6]

Curators face the difficult task of honoring the professional (and sometimes conflicting) standards of various professional disciplines; using good judgment about the acquisition, care, and use of oral histories; and doing it all with limited resources. Ethical decisions must be made on a case-by-case basis, and in consultation with interviewers, project managers, legal experts and administrators. Here are some areas where ethics and judgment come into play.

Acquisition

The curator's first ethical decision is whether to accept the oral history collection at all. The mission of an archive is to preserve, manage and provide access to "historical and documentary records of enduring value."[7] Therefore, to accept materials that the archive cannot preserve and manage in a timely way is a violation of the Society of American Archivists' *Code of Ethics*.

It is always best when a relationship with a repository is established by the oral historian before interviews begin. This way the requirements of the archive can be incorporated into the oral history project design and the legal rights can be transferred directly to the archive. (See also Chapter 2: Archives Administration, Acquiring an Oral History Collection.)

Conflict of Interest

Sometimes the goals of donors conflict with the mission of the archive, and of the profession. This issue can get complicated when a donor offers an exciting collection with conditions attached, or a philanthropist offers funds to digitize oral histories on one side of an issue but not the other. But the standards of oral history, archives, and library professions are clear: Never compromise intellectual freedom or open and equal access to any materials in your collections.

Monitoring *Content* of Oral Histories

Interview content can have both legal and ethical consequences for the archive. Sometimes a narrator says something about another person that could be considered injurious to his or her character (defamation) or could reveal intimate facts about another person (invasion of privacy). These are examples of legal torts in which the narrator, interviewer, and archive could be accountable in the event of a lawsuit.[8] This kind of litigation is rare in oral history, but something to be aware of.

Practice varies widely regarding how much oral historians or archivists review interview materials before they are deposited into the archive. Some listen to every recording and read every transcript before making it available to the public. More commonly, they ask narrators to review the interview and approve the content. Still others have no review at all. There is a fine line between monitoring the content of interviews for legal vulnerability and censoring the content. Every archive must find a workable balance.

Monitoring *Use* of Oral Histories

Barbara Sommer and Mary Kay Quinlan capture the curator's dilemma: "Some archivists and project managers [believe] that access to the material should be controlled. They argue that researchers . . . ought to explain their purpose when seeking permission to use or quote from such materials. [For many, this] comes close to censorship, . . . but concerns about censorship may take a back seat to the conviction that holders of oral history materials have an ethical obligation to assure that the narrators whose words are used will not be exploited, and that they will have a chance to benefit from possible commercial applications of oral history materials."[9] Most archives believe they have little control over how their materials are used, hoping that users will act in good faith and follow the instructions in the archive's written permission-to-quote form. The best balance between censorship and control lies in user education.

Respecting Cultural Values

William Schneider has given a great deal of thought to the cultural values of the narrator in his work with the native peoples of Alaska. The line is fuzzy between respecting the intent of a narrator and the culture he represents, and the responsibilities of a curator to make materials available. Schneider explains the dilemma: "On the one hand, the archive is asked to be sensitive to local interests about how a recording should be managed, and to know the interviewee's and interviewer's original intent and sentiment in creating a public record. I must continually remind myself that stories, even stories on tape, are not resources to be mined for information. . . . On the other hand, as a public office, the archive must secure its legal position so it has rights to make recordings available to all future users. . . . At the same time, we find it necessary to be as clear as possible about what a public facility can and can't do."[10] This is a subjective and sensitive issue and the curator's best tool is respect, sensitivity, and cultural awareness.

Oral Histories on the Internet

This is a rapidly changing frontier on two fronts. On one hand, as technology evolves, we have more opportunities to deliver information to a wider audience. On the other hand, as access broadens, so does the potential for misuse of information. Geoff Froh, technical manager for Denshō's digital archive, speaks from real-life experience: "Archivists are increasingly using the Internet to extend access to their oral history collections. They post not only finding aids, but full transcripts, full audio or video, often one linked to the other. No longer can we ignore the power of the Internet for access, and we can only speculate about the long-term consequences for universal access. At first, oral historians were timid about putting information on the Internet; now huge collections are being mounted. Access is almost always a good thing. I think the benefits outweigh the liabilities, but no matter what any of us think, the Internet is the wave of the future."[11] (See also Chapter 8: Oral Histories on the Internet.)

ETHICAL RESPONSIBILITIES

One of the purposes of professional associations is to lay out ethical standards for practitioners. Since curating oral histories is so interdisciplinary, I have drawn on the standards of the Oral History Association, the American Association for State and Local History, the American Historical Association, the Society of American Archivists, and the Alaska Native Knowledge Network to summarize the responsibilities of various constituencies working with oral histories. See the Resources section for links to the complete statements online.

Responsibilities of the Interviewer

INFORMED CONSENT. Interviewers should discuss the goals of oral history in general and of the particular project with the narrator, including the intended uses for the interview, the interview's final destination in an archive, and possibilities of electronic distribution. All the narrator's questions or reservations should be addressed honestly.

WRITTEN LEGAL CONSENT. Interviewers should have the narrator sign a legal consent form which clearly states the conditions of the interview, the rights of the narrator, and what will happen to the interview.

INTERVIEW PREPARATION. Interviewers should research the subject of the interview and the historical context surrounding it. Research can include conversations with other individuals, photographs and maps, as well as written materials. The interviewer should master the use of recording equipment.

RESPONSIBILITY TO NARRATOR. Interviewers should work to achieve a balance between the objectives of the project and the perspectives of the narrator. Interviewers must respect the rights of narrators not to discuss certain subjects, to tell a story in their own words, to restrict access to the interview, or to request anonymity.

OBJECTIVITY. Interviewers should not let personal biases show during the interview. They should be sensitive to the diversity of social and cultural experiences and to the implications of race, gender, class, ethnicity, age, religion, and sexual orientation.

RESPONSIBILITY TO SPONSORING INSTITUTION. Interviewers must realize that they are the public face of the institutions they represent: the oral history program, academic institution, and the funding organization. Not only must they comply with the stated policies of each institution, but they must also conduct themselves in such a way befitting the institution itself.

Responsibilities of the Oral History Program

SOCIAL RESPONSIBILITY. Oral history programs should design projects that cover the breadth of cultural experiences and perspectives of the community studied. They should include members of the community in planning, and involve them as much as possible in program activities. They should ensure that program objectives include ways to share the results of the oral history project with the community participants.

RESPONSIBILITY TO THE NARRATOR. Program guidelines should explicitly state the legal, ethical, and cultural standards regarding individual privacy, human-based research, and the use of sensitive topics, paying particular attention to communities that have traditionally been underrepresented. Interviews should remain confidential until narrators have given final approval. Good faith efforts should be made to ensure that the uses of the recordings and transcripts comply with both the letter and the spirit of the narrator's wishes.

INTERVIEWER TRAINING. It is the program's responsibility to train interviewers in program goals; interview techniques; legal, ethical, and cultural considerations in oral history; and use of recording equipment. Training should include information specific to the communities studied, especially in regard to cultural background of participating groups.

INTERVIEW INTEGRITY AND CONTEXT. The original recording must never be altered. However, if editing, excising, or rearranging of interview material is done for any reason in either the recording or the transcript, this action must be recorded, including by whom, when, and why.

ARCHIVING. Oral history projects should establish a relationship with an archive that will catalog, preserve, and provide access to interview materials in a timely way. The requirements of the archive regarding legal papers, labeling, and interview summaries should be incorporated into the program's procedures. It is the oral history project's responsibility to make sure interview materials are delivered to the archive in a timely way and according to the collecting policies of the archive.

Responsibilities of the Archive

ACCESSIONING. Archivists should use good judgment in acquiring oral history collections, and not accept collections they are not able to process and make available for use in a timely manner.

ACCESS. Archivists should promote open and equitable access to their collections without discrimination or preferential treatment, in accordance with cultural sensitivities, institutional policies, and legal requirements. They should strive to extend access beyond the walls of the repository through exhibitions, tours, educational programs, publications, and online distribution.

PRIVACY. Archivists should respect the privacy of donors, users, creators, and subjects of oral histories. Furthermore, archivists should respect the confidentiality of records in their custody and recognize all legal, social, and cultural restrictions to access.

LEGAL ISSUES. Archivists should become familiar with and uphold all federal, state, and local laws and statutory requirements pertaining to custody of oral histories.

COLLECTION MANAGEMENT. Archivists must follow best practices for the physical care and management of oral history materials, and always act to preserve their physical integrity. Cataloging, finding aids, and other record-keeping systems should be used to track both the processing activities and the content of oral histories.

PRESERVATION. Archivists should be aware of the complexities involved with the physical care, storage, and preservation of oral histories, and should stay abreast of developments and best practices for managing these materials. They should apply the same high standards for the care of oral histories that they apply to their other collections.

THE BOTTOM LINE

Fortunately, most of us will not brush against the law in our jobs as curators, but having the proper written documentation is the best way to avoid problems. Since ethical issues are always unique, curators must use common sense, sensitivity, institutional precedent, and professional codes of ethics to make the best decision in every situation. Remember to:

• Get everything in writing.

• Document any variation to established practice.

• Make sure your legal release agreements fit your program.

• Educate yourself and your staff in the law.

• Consult with legal advisors and administrators in legal and ethical issues.

Useful Forms in Appendix B

Basic Consent Form

Sample Consent Form

Sample Interviewer Gift to Archive

Sample Deed of Gift to the Public Domain

Sample Consent to Publish

Sample Consent to Publish on the Internet

Sample Online Site Use Agreement

CHAPTER 4

RECORDING TECHNOLOGY

Patiently waiting for a technology to mature does not make you a Luddite. It makes you technologically responsible.

—Doug Boyd

Love it or hate it, we definitely cannot ignore it. Technology plays an increasing role in our jobs, and will for some time to come, as we collectively move from an analog to a digital world. As curators, our primary interest in recording technology is in the results of it— the discs, tapes, and other media that come into the archive, though some of us may be responsible for recording equipment, as well.

This chapter introduces recording technology from a curator's point of view. The field is complex and constantly changing, so my generalizations are bound to be a bit outdated, even in the time it takes for this book to go to press. For this reason, I urge you to check the Resources section at the end of this book for pointers to the most up-to-date information online.[1] Be sure to check also Chapter 7: Preservation, which addresses technology from a preservation point of view.

THE BASICS

Recording technology is a tool for getting the job done; it shouldn't be a job in itself. Keep these thoughts in mind as you work with it.

- Built-in technology obsolescence is a fact of life in this rapidly evolving field. Don't worry if you can't keep up. We're all in the same boat.

- Best practices for *recording* are different from best practices for *preservation*. Since both involve technology, it is easy to mix them up, but curators should be careful to separate these distinct functions in planning and administering their collections.

- A digital environment means a new mindset. New standards and protocols are required for accessioning, cataloging, storing, and providing access to digital files. For example, the distinction between *original* and *copy* is less significant; the *content* of the recording must be considered separately from the **recording medium**; and a digitally recorded interview can arrive in the archive **media independent**, for example, as a sound file sent to the archive over the Internet.

- No solution is perfect and no solution is forever. Be prepared to **refresh** data, replace equipment, and revise procedures as technologies change, but use common sense about matching recording technologies to your needs. Stay aloof from the fads and commercial promotions, and implement new technologies only when they further your goal.

- Make recording technology your slave, not your master.

SORTING OUT THE TERMS
Audio vs. Video

Oral histories have been conducted exclusively as audio recordings until recently. In fact, the

Figure 4.1. Oral History and Recording Technology: Uncomfortable Bedfellows

Oral history practice has developed hand-in-hand with the evolution of recording technology. The first recorded oral histories were conducted in the military during World War II, but oral history found a welcome home in academia shortly thereafter. Early interviews were conducted on bulky, open-reel tape recorders, then transcribed, and the transcript was deposited into an academic library for the use of scholars. The transcript, not the recording, was considered the primary document. In fact, tapes were often discarded, or erased and reused.

The 1960s and 1970s were a prolific time for oral history, thanks to the introduction of the portable tape recorder. This inexpensive and user-friendly recorder made it easy to conduct field interviews, and affordable for individuals and small organizations to undertake oral history projects. Audiocassettes are small, well packaged, and affordable. Interviews conducted during this period were usually transcribed and deposited into an archive, along with the recording on audiocassette. Less thought was given at that time to audiocassettes' limited lifespan, and it didn't matter much anyway, because the transcript was still considered the primary document, and the recording was the backup. Most interviews in repositories today were recorded on audiocassettes.

Oral history practice reached another milestone in the mid-1990s, when digital audio technology came into its own. While the portable tape recorder opened doors for conducting oral histories, digital technology opened doors for preserving and presenting them. The ease of indexing, editing, and manipulating digital files, combined with a new generation of tech-savvy subject specialists, offered a new arena for bringing oral history to a wider audience through digital storytelling, online galleries, and digital archives.

About the same time, oral historians began exploring video as a recording medium, coining the term *visual history*. Video obviously enriches the interview by offering a visual portrait of the narrator, and his physical surroundings. Video is increasingly popular as the technical barriers are removed.

Digital technologies are opening up opportunities for oral historians in recording, for archivists in preservation, and for a broader user community. Museum curators, documentary makers, educators, and performing artists have discovered how the spoken word can enliven their work, and have incorporated oral histories into their creative endeavors.

---

oral history field has developed around the idea of capturing the *voices* of narrators. But video is increasingly popular among oral historians, and has the obvious advantage of capturing the visual experience of the interview as well as the audio. Curators will see more visual histories come into the archive, and must prepare for their cataloging, storage, preservation, and access needs.

Analog vs. Digital

These two recording methods work very differently. **Analog** attempts to capture the complete sound wave, exactly as it occurs in nature. **Digital** captures samples of the sound wave in close intervals. Because of other recording factors, digital is currently considered better quality than analog for voice recordings. Figure 4.3 (p. 44) compares the two.

File Format vs. Medium vs. Content

We didn't think much about these distinctions in the old days, but in a digital environment it is essential to be clear about the differences. The **file format** (e.g., .wav, .pdf, .txt) tells a computer how to read it; the physical *medium* (CD, DVD, cassette) is the device it is recorded or stored on; and the *content* refers to the words of the speaker. The goal is to preserve the content, and this may require transferring it from one medium to another, and one file format to another.

Recording Media

These are the physical devices that carry the recorded interview—the discs and tapes that come into the archive. Recording media can be magnetic or optical, analog or digital, and there are fine distinctions even within these categories.

MAGNETIC TAPE. Tape is made of magnetic oxide, a binding agent, and plastic tape. The lifespan and preservation needs of tape vary enormously, depending on its age, the manufacturer, its composition, and how it has been cared for. Higher quality tape is also used for long-term storage in large facilities. Curators may need to learn the chemical composition of the tape, and how it was cared for in the past, to make a true assessment of its preservation needs.

Since the majority of oral histories in archives today are on magnetic tape, archivists must deal with this medium long after the rest of the world has gone digital. Many tapes in archives are coming to the end of their life. Though magnetic tape doesn't have a future in the recording world, it has an overwhelming presence in the archive.

OPTICAL MEDIA. Optical media store digital data, such as sound or images, captured by burning tiny pits on a disc with a laser. CDs,

---

Figure 4.2. Terminology Note

Analog and *digital* refer to methods of recording.

Tape and *disc* refer to the medium the recording is made or stored on.

We often associate tape with analog and disc with digital, and indeed they often line up this way, but this is not a direct correspondence and it is important to separate them in our thinking.

DVDs, and MiniDiscs are common optical storage media. This technology has not been around long enough to be evaluated for longevity; however, the life-span of the physical medium (as opposed to the content) is not as important since periodic **data migration** must be part of every digital preservation plan.

SOLID-STATE MEMORY. Sometimes called flash memory, this newer technology contains no moving parts and stores data, such as sound or images, directly to a computer memory chip. Digital camera cards and USB flash drives are examples. Many digital field recorders are beginning to use this technology as capture media, rather than tape or optical disc. It is easy to transfer data from solid-state memory, and it is also compact; however, it is still fairly expensive.

OLDER MEDIA. Some recording media never made it to the mainstream or have become obsolete, such as wire and wax cylinder media, DAT, and microcassette. Oral histories recorded on these media will become increasingly problematic for archives as the media deteriorates and playback equipment becomes obsolete. These oral histories could be at serious risk and should be reviewed by a preservation expert and transferred to another medium.

Figure 4.3. Analog vs. Digital*

ANALOG	DIGITAL
• Captures the entire sound wave.	• Captures samples of the sound wave.
• Sound quality degrades with each generation of copying.	• No loss in quality with copies.
• Sound quality is limited, especially regarding speed variation and noise.	• Sound quality is dependent upon equipment, but generally superior to tape recording.
• Very fault-tolerant: if media is damaged, you can still hear it, even if at lower fidelity.	• Capture is all or nothing. If something is amiss, you lose it all.
• Uses a low-tech mechanical machine for recording and playback.	• Requires sophisticated machinery to record and play back.
• Lifespan of magnetic tape known to be limited.	• Lifespan of recording media is unknown.
• Tape is fragile—it crinkles and stretches.	• Recording media inexpensive and generally robust.
• Tapes and tape recorders are getting harder to purchase.	• No standard for file formats or recording media.
	• Allows for tracking, editing, and random access.
	• Format matters! Be aware of proprietary vs. open-source, compressed vs. uncompressed.

*Adapted from George Blood's "Planning an audio preservation transfer project," presented at the Society of American Archivist's Conference, 2002, rev. 2005. Online at http://www.safesoundarchive.com/PDF/AudioPreservProjectPlanning.pdf.

RECORDING EQUIPMENT

The variety of recording tools is truly astounding, and the choices are expanding all the time as new technologies emerge and older ones fade away. Most interviewers, however, just want something that is simple to use and will do the job well.

Recording Unit

A recording unit consists of three basic components:

RECORDER/PLAYBACK MACHINE. This is what does the recording. It can be audio or video, analog or digital, stationary or portable, simple or complex, inexpensive or very expensive. Most of the time the recorder can double for playback.

MICROPHONE. A **microphone** is a device that converts sound to an electrical signal so it can be captured by the recorder. Most recorders have built-in microphones, but oral historians always recommend using an external one. In fact, the quality of the microphone and its placement are considered the most important criteria in the sound quality of an interview. External microphones can be stereo or mono, dynamic or condenser, mono- or omni-directional, clip-on or desktop, and they vary a great deal in cost.

Figure 4.4. Audio vs. Video for Oral Histories*

Commitment to video is about choice, preference, and outcome. One is not an inherently better interviewing tool than another—just a different one. Though video gives you the choice of using video *and* audio, it requires far greater technical and financial resources to maintain than the audio recording. If you have those resources, by all means use video if you so desire. Video technologies are advancing so that production quality is excellent, and the capture technology is easy, accessible, and affordable. It adds the visual dimension that can be so meaningful and powerful in the interview experience.

At this time, however, a blind commitment to video technology could drive a well-off archive into bankruptcy. Digital formats are very expensive to preserve appropriately. Many of my early (5 years old) Mini-DV tapes are degrading, even though they are well cared for. DVD has not emerged as a preservation solution for a myriad of reasons. Technologies are on the horizon that will make the preservation of uncompressed video more accessible and affordable, but for now audio is so much more stable and affordable. Patiently waiting for a technology to mature does not make you a Luddite. It makes you technologically responsible.

We have launched a searchable database at the Kentucky Oral History Commission website that delivers the audio/video and transcriptions over the Internet. Granted, it's the video that draws viewers to our website, but this is because the video is professional quality. Just because someone buys a fancy digital video camera does not guarantee this look. This look is dependent on the fact that we had lights, professional videographers, controlled environment, and multiple camera angles — conditions that would have been cost prohibitive had we used video for every interview.

We have plenty of examples of video histories in our archive that weren't conducted in a controllable environment, where the lighting is poor, the narrator is obviously self conscious and won't make eye contact—video interviews that, despite their digital origins, are far below professional standards/public perception of what is viewable. Are these inherently better for the historical record just because they were video born digital?

Dr. Douglas Boyd
Program Manager,
Kentucky Oral History Commission

*Posting to H-ORALHIST, 13 December 2005.

RECORDING MEDIA. These devices—the cassettes, discs, and reels that carry the sound—are what archivists are most concerned with. Each medium is designed for a particular kind of recorder. Remember that the medium that is used for recording is not necessarily the best for preservation.

Purchasing Equipment

Base decisions about purchasing recording equipment on the needs, goals, and resources of your project, not on the newest and fanciest technology. Begin by answering these questions:

- Will interviews be recorded in audio or video? (Video is more expensive and technically complex, so it is important to justify this from the beginning.)
- Who will use the equipment, and how comfortable are they with technology? What kind of training is needed? Will interviewers or a technician operate the equipment?

- What is the projected timeframe for using the equipment? Is it a single, short project or an ongoing oral history program?

- How will equipment be used? Will interviews be conducted in a field or studio situation? Indoors or outdoors? Used by many people or just a few?

- Do you anticipate special recording needs, such as narrators with soft voices, group interviews, music recording, or poor acoustic environments?

- How will the oral histories be used? Will the sound be broadcast over the Internet or the radio, or will interviews go directly into the archive?

- What is the budget for equipment? Is it a one-time opportunity for purchasing or are ongoing funds available for equipment refreshment?

Answers to these questions should provide enough information to draft specifications for your equipment needs. To learn about the specific models of recorders and microphones, read reviews on the Internet, talk to colleagues with similar projects, post queries on online discussion groups, and check product specifications on manufacturers' websites to find products to suit your needs. Then you are ready to buy.

Assembling a Recording Kit

A good way to manage recording equipment for a project is to assemble kits containing everything an interviewer will need during an interview. Include a log book, so interviewers can record problems with the recorders, and notes for future interviewers. Figure 4.5 lists the items in a sample recording kit. Be sure to establish a system for tracking each kit, so you know who is using it at any time.

Check the kit on a regular basis to verify that none of the components is missing, that the default settings on the recorder or micro-

Figure 4.5. Sample Recording Kit

- Recorder
- Microphone
- Extension cord
- Headphones
- Recorder user manual
- Microphone user manual
- Log book
- Spare batteries
- Spare recording media

These items easily fit into a carrying case for field interviewers.

phone are correct, and that the log book notes any problems that should be attended to.

Keeping Track of Equipment

Be sure to keep track of information about recording equipment: purchase date, serial number, vendors, service contract or warranty, known problems, and a schedule for regular maintenance. This can be done on a database, spreadsheet, or with paper files, and the small amount of work to do this will be amply repaid if anything goes wrong.

Maintaining Equipment

Recording equipment does not require much maintenance, but it should be checked on a regular basis. It's rare that anything goes wrong, but if it does, the consequences are disastrous. Check the batteries in microphones and recorders. These need to be refreshed or recharged periodically, whether or not they are used. The procedure varies, depending upon the unit, the kind of batteries used, and how much use they get. Find out if the microphone has its own battery, and if it does, replace this battery as well. Also, magnetic tape recorders tend to get "magnetized" with use and this degrades the recording quality. If you use a magnetic tape recorder, demagnetize the tape heads from time to time.

THE BOTTOM LINE

Generally, recording technology (as opposed to preservation technology) forms only a small part of a curator's job. Since the choices for recording interviews are both vast and constantly evolving, it is counterproductive to try to keep up with the field, except where it intersects with your immediate needs. Keep the following in mind as you work with recording equipment:

- The microphone is the most important component of the recording unit.
- The interviewer's skill with the recording equipment is more important than the kind of recording equipment.
- Best practices for recording are different from best practices for preservation.
- Digital technology is the present and the future. If you are purchasing new recording equipment, consider digital recorders.
- Video has many advantages, but it comes with a price.

CHAPTER 5

TRANSCRIBING

Everyone knows that there are worlds of meaning that lie beyond words; nobody pretends . . . that the transcript is in any real sense a better representation of reality than the voice itself. Meaning inheres in context and setting, in gesture, in tone, in body language, in expression, in pauses, in performed skills and movements. To the extent we are restricted to text and transcription, we will never locate such moments and meaning, much less have the chance to study, reflect on, learn from and share them.

—Michael Frisch

In the mid-20th century, when the field of oral history was young, interviews were recorded, transcribed, often bound, and deposited into the archives of great universities. Print was the unquestioned medium for scholarly work, and there was no reason for oral historians not to follow this model. Nobody questioned the transcript as the primary document, and it wouldn't matter anyway, because recordings were often discarded or not made available for public use.

But those days have passed. Transcription is expensive and labor intensive, and besides, advances in recording technology, sound editing, and playback make it easy for users to skip from topic to topic as they would in a printed transcript.

So why transcribe an interview at all? Isn't that going backwards? A good question, and one that oral historians are actively discussing. Nevertheless, transcribing interviews remains standard practice for most oral history programs that can afford it, and there are good reasons for doing so.

This chapter examines these issues from a curator's point of view—the pros and cons of transcribing, what it involves, and how to plan for your own institution.

ABOUT TRANSCRIBING

What Is a Transcript?

Theoretically, a transcript is a verbatim version of the spoken word, analogous to a translation from one language to another. In reality, an exact reproduction of the spoken word is impossible. Judgments about punctuation and paragraphs must be made when transferring sound to paper. Sometimes user tools such as table of contents, chapter headings, or indexes are included, as well as photographs, maps, and historical and biographical materials. Though these tools are helpful to users, each one adds the thumbprint of an editor, and the transcript becomes a derivative work instead of a verbatim rendering of the recording.

In other words, not all transcripts are the same, and curators should take note of just what they are getting in a transcript. They should document what the transcript includes, and how it represents or deviates from the recording.

Transcribing Pros and Cons

Much is lost in transferring a unique voice and speaking style to the flatness of print on a page,

Figure 5.1. The Transcription Question

PROS	CONS
• Clarifies difficult-to-understand sections of the recording.	• Can be misleading. Cannot capture sarcasm, irony, and other nuances of speech.
• Is easy to edit and document changes through the use of footnotes, hand-written annotations, or strikeouts.	• Can discourage listening or viewing.
• Provides correct spelling of proper names.	• Is expensive in labor and time.
• Can be used as an index to the audio.	• Is one more item for archivist to process, store, and catalog.
• Is user-friendly—easy to browse and doesn't need special equipment.	• Is less necessary in the digital age.
• Is the ultimate preservation format.	

so much so that the result can be misleading. The audio recording provides the listener with not only the narrator's story, but also his unique way of telling it—repetitions, pauses, laughter and tears, distractions in the room, interactions with the interviewer, and unique speaking patterns. None of these nuances can be effectively transferred to the printed page.

On the other hand, the transcript is effective in conveying the intellectual content of the interview. A carefully prepared transcript with accurate spelling of proper names, verified dates and places, and a transcription of hard-to-understand sections of the audio interview provides important benefits that are lost in the recording.

Transcripts serve two additional functions for the archivist: preservation and access. Paper is the single most stable preservation medium and is always the ultimate backup. It requires no machinery to read, is lightweight, durable, and easily transported. And when it comes to user preference, the paper transcript almost always is the first choice.

But times are changing rapidly and the possibilities for manipulating digital data are forcing oral historians to reevaluate the cost/benefit ratio of transcribing. As Michael Frisch predicts, "one way or another . . . it is going to be more and more feasible to hear, see, browse, search, study, refine, select, export, and make use of extracts from oral histories directly—through engaging the documentation itself. In the future that is rapidly unfolding, I can claim with considerable confidence, this mode . . . will become the primary, preferred way to explore and use oral history."[1]

Who Transcribes

Transcribing is an art and craft that requires skill and judgment, and the transcriber should be included in the oral history team. Transcription can be done by the interviewer, a staff member, or a professional agency. There are advantages and disadvantages to each.

INTERVIEWER. In many ways the interviewer is most qualified to transcribe the interview. As the person best acquainted with the narrator and the subject matter, the interviewer can draw upon the interview experience for deciphering hard-to-understand sections, and recall the context of the interview as she types.

Figure 5.2. Qualities of a Good Transcriber

- Accurate typing
- Attention to detail
- Subject background
- Accurate speller
- Adept in using transcribing equipment
- Expert with word-processing programs

STAFF MEMBERS. Sometimes staff members or volunteers transcribe interviews. In-house transcription has several advantages: it saves the expense of **outsourcing**; staff members have a commitment to the project and in-depth knowledge of the topic; and there is usually close communication among the interviewer, archivist, and transcriber. The disadvantage is that staff members may not have the time to transcribe, and the project ends up on the back burner.

PROFESSIONAL TRANSCRIBER. The third choice is to outsource transcription to a free-lance transcriber or an agency. Professional transcribers are skilled at what they do, but the curator must provide detailed instructions. Most oral historians who have used professional transcribers have been happy with the results and have found it cost effective, especially for large collections.

Alternatives to Transcribing

If you choose not to have interviews transcribed, there are other options. Here are some tools oral historians can use in place of transcription.

INTERVIEW SUMMARIES. A few paragraphs describing the content of the interview is one of the best and least expensive tools for providing quick access. It is best done by the interviewer, and many oral history projects require that the interviewer submit a written summary with the recording. The summary can be re-used in catalog records, finding aids, reports to administrators, and publicity.

TAPE LOGS. A **tape log** is a list of topics indexed by timed intervals from the audio tape. This tool is extremely helpful to researchers using tape-recorded interviews, since they can fast-forward to the relevant sections without scanning the entire tape. Tape logs were common practice when audiotape was the standard for recording oral histories, and many useful tape logs accompany oral histories in archives today. However, the tape log is bound to the actual tape because of time-linked indexing, and its value is greatly compromised if the sound recording is missing, edited, or transferred to another format.

INDEXING DIGITAL FILES.[2] One of the wonders of digital sound files is the ability to index the content and mark tracks, as in a music CD. Sound editors can insert track marks with annotations or can actually link the sound to a corresponding section of the transcript. This new technique offers enormous opportunities for oral historians, and is likely to become standard practice in the future.

Beyond "Tape to Type"

Once the typing is done and the transcript is in electronic form, a number of steps can be taken to verify, enhance, or improve it. Here are some common post-transcript steps:

VERIFYING CONTENT

AUDIT-CHECK. After the interview is transcribed, it needs to be **audit-checked**, that is, proofread by listening with the transcript on the screen, so transcription errors can be corrected.

Though this task is often assigned to the transcriber, I find that the interviewer is best qualified to audit-check. With the interview experience fresh in mind, she can recall hard-to-decipher sections and correct transcriber errors at the same time.

VERIFYING FACTS. Oral historians often acknowledge the difference between memory and the written record by noting discrepancies such as dates, places, and events. These annotations are helpful to users, but they should be made as footnotes or enclosed in brackets in the text, not as changes to the transcript.

VERIFYING SPELLING OF PROPER NAMES. Correct spelling and format of proper names is essential for interviews going into an archive. Names of people, institutions, places, and events are an obvious point of access for users, and a slight spelling error will render that name useless. (This is increasingly important as we move to a digital environment which includes keyword-searching capabilities.) In addition, an error in a primary document will be repeated over and over in the catalog record, finding aid, and published works.

DOCUMENT STRUCTURE

CHAPTER AND SECTION HEADINGS, TABLE OF CONTENTS. Some oral historians organize the transcript into a book-like format, with a table of contents, chapters, and section headings. This kind of structuring enhances the usability of the transcript and is popular with readers; however, it imposes a third-party interpretation on the narrator's words.

INDEX. An index is an excellent tool to guide users directly to topics within the transcript or series of transcripts. The larger the body of material, the more useful the index, so it is more worthwhile to index larger oral history series or long oral histories than single interviews. Indexing is expensive since it requires the skills of a professional, and as electronic search options improve, the value of a print index must be weighed against the cost of creating it.

ACCOMPANYING MATERIAL. Some oral historians supplement the transcript with contextual material such as a project description, historical and biographical material, interviewer's notes, photographs and clippings. All of this information is useful for researchers, and is encouraged by the Oral History Association Evaluation Guidelines.

ALTERING THE TRANSCRIPT AT THE NARRATOR'S REQUEST. It is standard practice for the narrator to review the transcript, and to have the final word about the version that goes into the archive, and therefore into the public record. Some narrators sign off on the transcript without looking at it; others want to make a great many editorial changes and "clean it up." Interviewers should explain that the purpose of the review is to clarify facts or correct errors in the transcript, not to produce a polished document. Explain how important it is for the transcript to match the recording. This is best practice for both oral history and archives management, but if the narrator insists on making changes, his wishes must be honored. Changes to the transcript should be documented.

CORRECTING TEXT. Corrected names, dates, or other facts can be indicated within brackets in the body of the text, or as a footnote. In either case, it should be clear that the changes are deviations from the recording.

ADDING TEXT. Sometimes reading the transcript will jog the narrator's memory and he wants to add a fact or two, a story, or a whole new line of thought. There are several ways to accomplish this without altering the integrity of the transcript:

- Facts or short comments can be added as footnotes.
- A lengthy addition to a topic discussed in the interview can be placed as an addendum to the text.
- If the narrator wishes to explore a new topic, consider conducting another interview.

DELETING TEXT. Deleting text is problematic since once the transcript is altered, it no longer matches the recording. Generally, text should be deleted only in unusual circumstances—for example, if the narrator says something defamatory or reveals private information about another person.

Deleting text causes an additional problem for the archivist. If the narrator insists that material be deleted from the transcript (and therefore from the public record), then the recording must be restricted from public use. In the past, sections of tape were erased to accomplish this, but this is neither good archival practice, nor is it practical for large collections.

PUTTING THEORY INTO PRACTICE

Transcribing is an expensive and exacting task. It takes an experienced transcriber six to eight hours to transcribe a single recorded hour. That's when everything goes well. If the recording quality is poor, or the speakers are hard to hear, it takes more time. If the transcriber researches proper names, adds chapter headings, table of contents, or index, or audit-checks the transcript—even more time. As we all know, time translates into dollars.

The quality of a transcriber's work is dependent upon the material she has to work with—both the recording and the transcribing instructions. If the sound recording is flawed or if the speaker is hard to understand, the transcriber must guess or leave sections out. If the instructions are not clear about formats, method of delivery, style, and appropriate software, she must contact the curator to verify instructions. The more questions that arise during the transcription process, the more room for error. This usually translates to more follow-up, more time, and more expense.

This is why it is important to plan carefully how to handle transcription for your project. This section suggests a three-step planning process. Use or adapt the worksheets in Appendix B to organize your thinking.

Step 1. Plan for Transcribing

This is the time to brainstorm. Think about your transcribing goals, and the resources you have to accomplish them. The questions in the *Transcribing Plan* will guide your thinking. Compare your answers to the comments below, then move to Step 2.

COLLECTION. Will you be transcribing a backlog? A new collection? Is there ongoing transcription work, or a single series of interviews? Each scenario poses different issues and different solutions.

PREPARATION. Transcribing should be done from *copies* of the original recording, especially if the transcribing is done off-site. Current transcription equipment will handle only standard audiocassettes (transcription machine) or digital files (digital transcription software). The original recording should be copied to a medium or file format appropriate to the transcribing equipment—audiocassette or digital file. Copying is a time-consuming step that requires special equipment and a certain amount of skill.

EXTENT. Consider both the duration (number of recorded hours) and the number of physical items (reel, cassette, disc, or sound file). The total number of recorded hours will give you a ballpark figure for estimating costs and time required. The number of physical items will help you estimate figures for handling, format transfer if necessary, and storage.

WORKFLOW/TIMEFRAME. What is the deadline for completion of the project? What is the turnaround time for individual transcripts? How will the recording and transcript be delivered to and from the archive? Who will do the work? How will you deliver and receive materials from transcribers? Is the archive providing transcription equipment? Computer and office space for transcribers? All these questions need to be addressed in your plan.

RESOURCES. Allocating resources for transcribing is a balance between money and people/ technology. A project short on funds might look to volunteers to do the transcribing. But an archive with a large collection of recordings may seek a grant to have them transcribed by an outside agency. The curator's job is to make the very best use of the resources at hand.

ADDITIONAL TASKS AND SUPPLEMENTARY MATERIAL. Think about the final product. What additional tasks should the transcriber do? The oral historian?

OBSTACLES? Are there known sections of the recording that are of poor quality? Are narrators difficult to understand on tape? Are there foreign words or phrases? These obstacles will slow down the transcription. If possible, curators should identify problems ahead of time and alert the transcriber.

Step 2. Develop a Transcriber's Protocol

The curator is responsible for ensuring that transcribers have the proper equipment and computer setup for transcribing; a quality copy of the recording; and proper instructions for style, formatting, and delivery of the transcript. She must also consider how, when, and where the work will be done, and how it will be paid for. A written protocol for transcribing should include all this information, and should be part of the archive's permanent documentation so it can be referred to over the years. Use or adapt the *Transcribing Protocol* in Appendix B to suit your own needs.

Figure 5.3. Sample Transcription Workflow

1. Archivist introduces interviewer to transcriber via email.

2. Interviewer delivers original recording to archivist.

3. Interviewer provides list of proper names and other special instructions to transcriber.

4. Archivist copies original recording and delivers the copy to transcriber.

5. Transcriber transcribes interview, sends electronic copy to interviewer and archivist. Transcriber keeps electronic copy until oral history is complete.

6. Interviewer audit-checks the transcript and makes corrections.

7. Interviewer sends transcript to narrator for approval, urges against changes except spelling or facts.

8. Interviewer makes any final corrections and sends a final electronic copy to archivist.

Figure 5.4. Things to Include in Transcription Instructions

- Format of recording (sound file or audiocassette).
- Specifications for formatting the document
- How to handle extraneous sounds in the room, laughter, "umms," and repeated words
- What to do about passages that can't be understood
- What to do about foreign words or phrases
- What to do about proper names if the spelling is unclear
- What is expected regarding proofreading, spellchecking, audit-checking
- Word processing program and version to deliver completed transcript
- Method of delivery (email attachment, disc, print copy)

Step 3. Develop Transcriber's Guidelines

The final document includes all the instructions the transcriber will need: contact information, style guide, computer specifications, and method of delivery. See sample *Transcribers Guide* in Appendix B.

Working with Existing Transcripts

Curators consider it a blessing when oral histories come into the archive already transcribed. But transcripts vary in quality, and curators should pay attention to exactly what they receive and how it relates to the recording.

PARTIAL TRANSCRIPTIONS. Researchers often conduct interviews and transcribe only the sections they need for their scholarly work, then donate these materials to an archive. Though this makes sense for the researcher, a partial transcript is not good archival practice. Since it does not reproduce the recorded interview, it can actually be misleading. If the archive has partially transcribed interviews, get full transcripts if possible. Otherwise, be sure to document that the transcript is incomplete.

TRANSCRIPT ONLY. Sometimes the recording is lost, or of such poor quality it can't be useful, and the transcript is the only document that comes to the archive. Lucky the interview was transcribed! This is fine, and the transcript can be accessioned into the archive without the recording. Just be sure to note this in the record-keeping system.

PAPER OR ELECTRONIC COPY. Until recently, transcripts were only kept on paper, but today they almost always arrive in electronic format for the archivist to print and bind. What about the electronic copy? There are a number of reasons to keep it—both on a server and on external medium such as CD: it's an additional backup copy, it can easily be transferred to a digital archive, and copies can be sent to other institutions or researchers.

THE BOTTOM LINE

Because of the inherent differences between sound and print, as well as the variety of practices among oral historians, the relationship between the transcript and the recording will always be problematic in the archive. The best way for an archivist to reconcile these differences is to document exactly what the transcript consists of and how it differs from the recording. Often this seems like excessive detail, but when you remember that archival materials and the record-keeping systems to track them must be useful to researchers into the indefinite future, the extra work is justified.

- Transcribing has many advantages, but is not absolutely necessary.
- Transcribe from a copy of the recording, not the original.
- Consider the transcript a preservation format.

- A transcript should match the recorded interview. Any differences between the two should be documented.
- The quality of the transcriber's work is dependent upon the quality of the materials she receives: the recording and the instructions.

Useful Forms in Appendix B

Transcribing Plan

Transcribing Protocol

Sample Transcribers' Guide

CHAPTER 6

CATALOGING

What is the difference between the trunk in Grandma's attic and a library? A catalog, of course!

Whether or not we've had to sort through the papers in Grandma's attic for that one elusive document, we all know that simply keeping documents is not enough to make the information in them available in any practical sense. There needs to be a structured system to organize the information, and that system must tell us both where the document is physically located and what information it contains. Obviously, the larger the pile of documents the more we depend on a system to organize their contents.

That's where cataloging comes in. No matter how simple or complex, good cataloging is grounded in three principles. First is *structure*. A catalog consists of certain clearly defined elements—the catalog itself, catalog records within it, and data fields within each record. Each unit within the hierarchy is clearly defined by cataloging rules. The second principle is *description*. A catalog record should describe the physical item, its intellectual contents, where it is physically located, and its relationship to similar items. The third principle is *analysis*. In order to direct users to the information they need, catalogers analyze the content of the item catalogued and add subject headings based on a **controlled vocabulary**. Overall, information for the catalog record must be accurate, precise, and consistently recorded.

Oral histories present a number of special problems for catalogers, and as a result recordings and transcripts all too often sit on the cataloger's problem shelf, forgotten or neglected. Some of these problems, such as multiple recording formats, are inherent to the nature of oral histories. Other problems arise because of misunderstandings between the oral historian and the cataloger about the nature of these materials, and who is responsible for what. Though the division of labor differs for each oral history project, a good way to think about the cataloging workflow is to consider the cataloger responsible for cataloging *structure*, and the oral historian responsible for its *content*.

This chapter introduces cataloging to novices, especially as it applies to oral histories, and offers suggestions for developing a catalog plan for your own project.

ORGANIZING INFORMATION

For a catalog to function, there must be an agreement or *standard* about what information is recorded, and the form in which that information is entered. In the past, it was sufficient for individuals or organizations to develop a local standard and stick to it. This is no longer true. With the potential for sharing catalog information, projects of any size—computerized or not—should design a catalog plan with universal standards in mind, so that cataloging can be shared, merged, and updated, now or in the future.

The Library Model

Librarians have been cataloging for many hundreds of years, perfecting protocols to connect books with interested users.[1] The library model is based on a single catalog record for a single published item, traditionally a book. Applying standards for recording data consistently is a fundamental principle for catalogers. For example, **Anglo American Cataloging Rules (AACR)**, **Functional Requirements for Bibliographic Records (FRBR)**, and **Resource Description and Access (RDA)** are standards for cataloging; **Dublin Core** and **EAD** are metadata schema for encoding bibliographic information; and **MARC (machine-readable cataloging) format** is a standard for exchanging catalog data electronically. Such standards make it possible for catalog records to be shared, to be exchanged among library catalogs, and to be easily understood by both catalogers and computers.

The Archives Model

Archival practice has developed parallel to, but until recently separately from, library practice. While librarians generally work with *single items* of *published* materials, archivists work with *collections* of *unpublished* materials. Archivists have traditionally described their collections by means of a **finding aid**, a detailed description of a collection and its contents. In recent years archivists have adapted MARC format to describe unpublished materials, and have added their holdings to library online catalogs (**OPACs**), blurring the distinction between library and archival practice.

The Internet Model

Organizing the vast and ever-changing information network on the Internet is a leap, many orders of magnitude, from the contained and easily defined library or archives catalogs. Information delivered via the Internet can come in many forms—sound, text, image, or database; the **address (URL)** can change at any time without notice; or visa versa, the content on a particular website can change at any time.

Information technologists and librarians are developing tools to organize the astronomical volume of information, connect it to an equally vast user base, and do it with precision. One of these organizing tools is **metadata**,[2] a protocol for data exchange which imposes structure on unstructured bits of information. Professional communities develop schema, or field tag definitions (analogous to MARC format for bibliographic description), for best describing their own materials in a web-based environment. EAD is the metadata scheme commonly used by archivists.

So where do oral histories fit into these disparate models? That's what all of us working in the field are asking. Neither fish nor fowl, oral histories have qualities of archival materials, sound recordings, visual recordings, and books. The respondents to my survey were fairly evenly divided among those who create finding aids, those who create MARC records, and those who don't catalog at all. Oral histories, indeed, have suffered from a lack of cataloging guidelines.

WHY CATALOG?

Good cataloging should accomplish all of the following tasks:

- **Organize materials.** A catalog organizes oral histories according to physical format, subject, project name, institution, geographical area, narrator's name and/or any other designated category.

- **Link to related items.** A catalog directs users to related materials about the person, topic, chronological period, narrator, or any other category designated by the cataloger.

- **Link description to physical item.** A catalog links descriptive information in the catalog record to the physical or virtual item(s) by means of an **address.** An address can be an **accession number**, a **call number**, or a **URL**.

- **Describe physical content.** A catalog record describes all the physical items which comprise the oral history—tapes, discs, transcripts—and how many of each.

- **Describe intellectual content.** A catalog record can include the names of the narrator and interviewer, biographical information, interview summary, subjects and proper names related to the content.

- **Provide multiple access points.** A catalog record enables users to find an oral history by the narrator's name, subject, oral history program, or any other term that catalogers choose to index.

- **Store administrative data.** A catalog record can also store administrative information important to staff, such as the donor's name, restrictions, physical locations, and instructions for permission to quote.

- **Share information across institutions.** Computer network-based cataloging allows users to access cataloging information from linked institutions in a single search.

CATALOGING CONCEPTS

Catalog Structure

No matter how large or small, simple or complex, a catalog consists of three increasingly detailed elements: the catalog, the catalog record, and the data field. This is true whether your catalog is a paper notebook, card catalog, standalone database, or library online catalog. Figure 6.1 shows this structure.

THE CATALOG. The catalog itself is the highest level in the hierarchy. It is the container for catalog records that are related in some way that makes it meaningful to search them as a group. Traditionally, a catalog represented all the holdings of a library, but today, thanks to standards for sharing data, catalogs can also be organized around the holdings of all the institutions in a region, a particular field of knowledge, or any other designated category.

THE CATALOG RECORD. The catalog record defines and describes the **bibliographic unit**

being cataloged—a single interview, multiple interviews of a person, or an entire oral history project. The cataloger and the oral historian determine what constitutes a bibliographic unit for a particular project. Decisions are based on the intent of the oral history project, the cataloger's time, and the level of detail they wish to achieve.

Catalogers make the distinction between **item-level** and **collection-level cataloging**.

ITEM-LEVEL CATALOGING. Generally, modern practices favor item-level cataloging because it provides better access to the materials. This method defines the bibliographic unit as a small intellectual unit—a single interview, or multiple interviews of the same person. Item-level cataloging is more time consuming than collection-level cataloging, since every item must be analyzed and described.

COLLECTION-LEVEL CATALOGING. The collection-level cataloging method is based on the archival finding aid, and describes an entire oral history collection in a single catalog record. This is most useful when there is a strong thread connecting many short interviews, such as a series of interviews about a single event.

Some catalogs provide both item-level records and collection-level records, with links from one to the other.

THE DATA FIELDS. The data fields that make up each catalog record contain the information about the oral history—the names of the narrator and interviewer, title, interview description, name of the oral history project, and other information you choose to include. It also provides a unique address to link it to the physical materials. In a computerized database, these fields can be individually defined with certain qualities, such as whether or not they are required, or whether or not they are indexed.

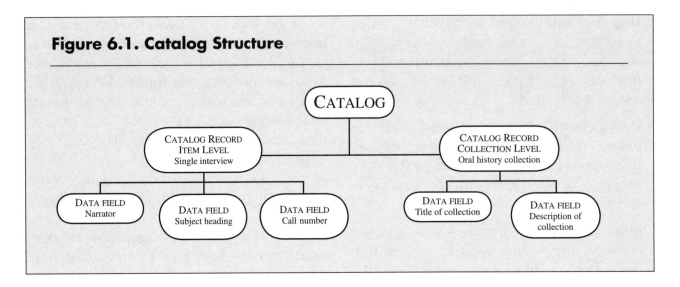

Figure 6.1. Catalog Structure

Standardized Vocabulary

Catalogers apply two principles regarding terminology, in order to help users find information quickly and consistently. The first principle involves a controlled vocabulary, mentioned earlier in this chapter. This principle states that for every proper name and topic, a single, unique term will be selected and applied consistently in catalog records. This is called a *controlled* or *authorized* term. The second principle involves relationships among these terms. Controlled terms are linked within the catalog by means of **cross references**, so that users can navigate among names and topics of interest. Cross references can be made to similar terms, broader or narrower terms, or variant forms of the same term.

Many controlled vocabulary lists already exist. The *Library of Congress Authorities*[3] is the most comprehensive, but others have been developed by specific disciplines to include specialized terminology. In most situations, it is the cataloger's job to apply controlled terms to the catalog record, based on the information provided by the oral historian. Often, the names and topics in an oral history are not in an existing list, so the oral historian and cataloger must develop a local controlled vocabulary to control terms specific to the project.

Once the vocabulary is established, catalogers will enter the controlled terms in the appropriate data fields in the catalog record, for example, one field is defined for the interviewer, another for the narrator, etc. In a library online catalog, the relationships among the controlled terms are linked, guiding users to related information.

Shared Cataloging

Sharing catalog records among institutions, digital archives, and library consortia is the best and least expensive way to provide access to a collection, and is the wave of the future. Oral history projects of any size should design a cataloging plan that applies standards and principles from the very beginning, so that catalog records can easily be shared. The benefits of sharing cataloging among institutions are enormous, and can only be achieved if the catalog record is delivered according to standards.

PUTTING THEORY INTO PRACTICE

Planning for cataloging requires collaboration among oral historians, catalogers, and sometimes technical experts and administrators. Follow the steps below, and use or adapt the worksheets in Appendix B to develop a plan that works best for your situation.

Step 1. Plan for Cataloging

Oral historians, curators, and catalogers should meet to discuss the project at hand, learn about each other's fields of expertise, and work out the large questions outlined below. The *Cataloging Plan* worksheet in Appendix B and the accompanying comments will help organize your ideas.

ACCESS TO LIBRARY. The first determination is whether or not your project has access to a library that is willing to manage the cataloging of your oral histories. If this is the case, then your job as oral historian or project manager is to establish an information flow between the project and the library, to ensure that catalogers receive complete and correct information about each item, and that you, as project manager, have the opportunity to check the cataloger's work. The library catalogers can do the actual cataloging, according to their own standards.

CATALOG HOME. If you establish a relationship with a library, your catalog records will very likely go into that library's online catalog, or OPAC. Most libraries also contribute records to a **bibliographic utility**, such as **OCLC**, to share cataloging with a very broad user base. Libraries can also share cataloging in regional or subject-specific catalogs, in order to extend access to specific user groups. If you are working with a library, be sure to discuss where the catalog records will reside, and the possibilities for sharing beyond the institution.

If you are not connected to a library, your catalog will very likely reside within your own organization. In this case, explore possibilities for getting broader exposure through sharing cataloging with similar institutions or posting cataloging on a website.

CATALOGERS. Librarian catalogers are highly trained in standards and procedures for cataloging, but may know less about the particular needs of oral histories, or of the subject matter of your collection. If this is the case, make sure to give them specific instructions about the content you want included in the catalog record, including a list of all proper names for the controlled vocabulary.

On the other hand, if volunteers or staff members catalog oral histories, they are probably experts in the subject matter and the needs of the project. In this case, use cataloging templates with specific instructions, so information will be entered consistently. The two cataloging worksheets in Appendix B are designed for these two situations.

COLLECTION. How do you want oral histories represented in the catalog? As a single collection record or as individual item records? What is the primary document to be catalogued: the audio or visual recording, or the transcript? If the oral history is part of a larger collection— for example, an author's personal papers—how do you want that represented? If oral histories are available online, do you want to link from the catalog record to the website? Answers to these questions will factor into the structure of the catalog record.

CONTENT. How detailed should cataloging be? Should biographical information and interview summaries be included? What terms should be indexed? How extensive should subject analysis be and who will do it? What are the parameters for a local controlled vocabulary? Are there names or terms that are unclear? If so, who will do the research to verify them? Answers to these questions determine the level of detail and the general quality of the catalog record. Adapt the cataloging worksheets in Appendix B to record and communicate data for the catalog record.

WORKFLOW/TIMEFRAME. What is the procedure for information flow between the oral history project and the catalogers? Will oral histories be catalogued in a single batch or over time? Approximately how many oral histories need to be catalogued each year/month? What is the expected turnaround time? These tricky details need to be agreed upon by all parties, whether the catalogers are in the same office or in a distant library, to ensure a smooth workflow and a reasonable turnaround time.

COSTS. What are the estimated costs for cataloging and who will pay for it? Costs can vary greatly, but are based on the level of detail, who does the cataloging, and exactly what is factored into it. There may also be technology expenses for software, hardware or subscription to a bibliographic utility.

SPECIAL REQUIREMENTS. Sometimes institutions—libraries, oral history projects, or administrative bodies—have requirements for cataloging, for example, required access points or the mention of a funding agency. Be sure to clarify this before you begin.

Step 2. Develop a Cataloging Protocol

Develop your planning discussions into a written statement, or cataloging protocol, which clearly defines the parameters of the cataloging project, and specifies the responsibilities of both the oral historians and the catalogers. Use or adapt the *Cataloging Protocol* worksheet in Appendix B to complete this step.

Step 3. Start Cataloging

Now it's time to begin cataloging. The specifications for the catalog have been established, so the cataloger simply needs the data to create the catalog records. Adapt either of the cataloging worksheets in Appendix B to your own needs. *Cataloging Worksheet #1* is most useful if the catalog record is entered by a student or volunteer, or when the cataloging is outsourced to an agency. In this case most of the description and analysis is done by the

person filling out the worksheet, and can be entered directly into a database. *Cataloging Worksheet #2* works best in a situation where the oral historian is recording information from an interview, so a professional cataloger can take over from there with the description and analysis. This worksheet assumes more technical skill for the cataloger.

CATALOGING ALTERNATIVES

Cataloging requires skill and technology, and that translates into time and money. Maybe it is not a priority for your project at this time. If this is the case, it is even more important to record the basic information (such as the information on each of the worksheets) about each interview accurately onto a printed form, a spreadsheet, or a collection management system. The sooner after the interview that the data is recorded, the better. This will ensure that, at least, the information will be accurately preserved, so a catalog record can be created at a later date.

Another common scenario is if a large collection of oral histories—a donation or a large backlog—will not fit into the general cataloging workflow. Outsourcing might be a good solution. Professional cataloging agencies generally provide high-quality cataloging and are cost effective. The planning worksheets in this book are useful tools to plan for outsourcing.

WHEN TO CONSULT AN EXPERT

Good cataloging can be done at any level based on the principles in this chapter. However, cataloging policy in a larger sense is increasingly driven by the demands and the extraordinary benefits of our interconnected world. Consider getting an expert opinion to make sure your plan will fill your institution's needs and comply with cataloging standards, especially if you undertake any of the following:

- Design a standalone database.
- Catalog oral histories in MARC format.
- Design a metadata scheme.
- Share cataloging in any form.
- Use catalog records for your website.

THE BOTTOM LINE

Oral histories may be difficult to catalog, but the overwhelming benefits always make it worthwhile. The quality of a catalog record is only as good as the information provided to the cataloger, and this must come from the person closest to the interview, usually the interviewer. If you are not able to catalog materials soon after the oral history is accessioned, then be sure to record the cataloging information completely and accurately on paper or a spreadsheet, so that it will be available when you can do more extensive cataloging.

- Work with the cataloger from the beginning of the oral history project.
- Provide the cataloger with correct and complete information.
- Catalog from worksheets or templates or from copies of the recording. Avoid using the original recording.
- Budget and plan for cataloging.
- Avoid backlog.

Useful Forms in Appendix B

Cataloging Plan
Cataloging Protocol
Cataloging Worksheet #1
Cataloging Worksheet #2
Sample MARC Record

CHAPTER 7

PRESERVATION

> Let us save what remains not by vaults and locks which fence them from the public eye and use . . . but by such a multiplication of copies, as shall place them beyond the reach of accident.
>
> —Thomas Jefferson

A CULTURAL HERITAGE IN CRISIS

- Audiocassettes account for more than 90 percent of the sound recordings in archives, and many of them are approaching the end of their ten- to thirty-year lifespan.

- Only 49 percent of audiovisual collections in archives are kept in a climate-controlled environment. The remaining 51 percent are kept in cardboard boxes, on open shelves, or in filing cabinets.

- Only 12 percent of libraries and archives with budgets under $10,000 reported making preservation master copies, and then only in some cases. Many respondents did not understand the difference between preservation copies, user copies, and original recordings.

- Only 18 percent of respondents have assessed the preservation needs of their audio collections.

These striking statistics are the findings of a survey conducted in 2000 by the American Folklore Society, the American Folklife Center of the Library of Congress, and the Society for Ethnomusicology,[1] to determine whether "the vast amount of folk heritage materials gathered by professionals for over half a century is entering safely into the cultural heritage of the nation."

This study was followed by another one, conducted in 2003 by the Council on Library and Information Resources (CLIR), to determine the state of audio recordings in eighty academic libraries. The institutions surveyed represent a sample of the United States' most elite and best-funded academic libraries, large and small. The conclusion: "The libraries and archives of the United States house a large and valuable heritage of audio recordings that span more than a century. . . . These rare and often fragile recordings are in triple jeopardy: they are frequently not described or inventoried; they are **orphaned** by obsolete playback equipment; and they clearly lack documented rights that allow use. Making these recordings available to students and scholars can be difficult and costly. As a result, these collections are often underused."[2]

The findings of these studies point to a cultural heritage in crisis. They corroborate the findings of my own survey and personal observations, and even though the two CLIR studies don't target oral histories, they include them in their findings. In fact, because oral history recordings are more likely to be housed in smaller, underfunded institutions (70 percent of my respondents represent institutions other than academic), their preservation needs are even more likely to be compromised.

❖

Preservation of older sound recordings is complicated and expensive, the learning curve is high, and while we are learning our collections continue to deteriorate. Our efforts are further confounded by the rapid evolution of digital preservation technology, which increases our options while at the same time renders earlier efforts obsolete. No wonder we are confused.

This chapter introduces the principles of preservation as they apply to oral histories, and offers tips for evaluating the preservation needs of your own collection. The subject matter naturally overlaps with the material in Chapter 4: Recording Technology, so don't hesitate to move back and forth between the two chapters. The most up-to-date information on this rapidly evolving field is on the Internet. Check the Resources section (Appendix D) for the best sources to begin your search.

THE BASICS

Preservation refers to the long-term care and protection of the *content* in archives. Applied to oral history, preservation should ensure that the spoken words in recorded interviews are available to users into the indefinite future, and lacking a recording, that the transcript will preserve the content of the interview on paper. Most preservation discussions focus on older materials in various stages of deterioration, including all the oral histories that were recorded on audiocassettes. This is a good thing, since so many of our materials are in danger of being lost forever. However, preservation policy can't end with doing triage on older materials; we must also plan now for the long-term preservation of our newer collections, in their various media and formats.

Digitization is bound to come up in preservation discussions. On one hand, digital formats are easier, more efficient, and in the long run, less expensive to manage. On the other hand, there is a huge and well-acknowledged gap between the enormous task of retrospectively digitizing our oral history collections, and the work we can actually accomplish with available resources. Who will digitize these collections? Where and how will digital files be stored? Who will be responsible for ongoing maintenance of the digital archive? Can we get it done in time, before the recording media deteriorates? Who will pay for it?

These are big questions for major universities, but they are overwhelming questions for the smaller institutions and community organizations that hold the majority of our cultural heritage.

Four Preservation Principles for Everyone

Much preservation work requires technical expertise and expensive equipment, but certain principles require nothing more than common sense. These four preservation principles can be applied to any oral history collection.

PHYSICAL ENVIRONMENT. In an ideal world, an archive consists of an onsite repository for user copies, as well as a permanent offsite storage facility for original and fragile materials, each with optimal environmental conditions for its contents. In real life, it's rare that an archive can achieve the perfect environment for all of its holdings, but attention to these principles goes a long way.

- Keep storage area dust- and insect-free.
- Keep temperature and humidity stable.
- Keep materials away from light.
- Handle only when necessary.
- Store in a secure vault to protect from theft, loss, or accidental misuse.
- Develop an emergency plan for natural disasters, such as flood or fire.

Copies. Keeping multiple copies of a document is an important preservation principle. Once a new recording comes into the archive, copy it immediately, and put the original into permanent storage. Use the new copy, called the **preservation master**, to make subsequent copies.[3]

Distribution. According to audio preservation consultant Elizabeth Cohen, "the key to preservation *is* distribution. . . . [O]ur collections are far more likely to survive if they are secure and robust in many hands."[4] Distribution of multiple copies is an important, easy, and often overlooked preservation principle. Copies in the different physical locations (and in different formats)—within an institution, across institutions, and in remote storage facilities—will safeguard the content from natural disasters and theft, as well as media deterioration and format obsolescence.

Transcript. It is unfortunate that the transcript does not often enter into preservation discussions, because it is the very best way to preserve the interview *content*. **Acid-free paper** is the ultimate preservation medium. It is easy to store, has a long shelf life, and doesn't require special equipment to read. Under the right conditions it can last for hundreds of years. Transcribing is considered an expensive step in processing an oral history, but when considered as a preservation tool among the other high-tech options, it weighs in as a great value.

Figure 7.1. Terminology Note: Recording Media

I take the shortcut of using the common term *recording media/medium* for any object that carries the sound or video, with the understanding that, technically, there are fine distinctions among recording, preservation, and storage media.

Understanding Recording Media

Chapter 4 offers an overview of recording media; this chapter builds upon that, as it applies to preservation. Figure 7.2 summarizes common recording media, and what you need to know about their preservation qualities.

Problems of Multiple Media. The oral histories in our collections today were recorded and archived on a variety of media—open-reel tape, audiocassette, DAT, etc. Each recording medium has unique requirements for preservation and storage. The more of them to manage, the more complicated the archivist's job. The practicalities of managing multiple media in their various sizes, shapes, and physical needs can be overwhelming for even the best equipped archive.

Obsolescence. Sound recordings on any media are subject to obsolescence for two reasons: unavailability of playback equipment or recording media, and new standards or technologies which supersede the old. For example, open-reel tapes are problematic because playback equipment is hard to find; and MiniDiscs have been made obsolete by newer technologies.

Commercial interests drive the built-in obsolescence of recording media, and the music industry introduces new recording devices like new car models. Interviewers, unfortunately, are at their mercy. These difficulties are passed on to archivists, who must accession, process, store, and preserve each new recording medium and format that comes into the archive.

Entering the Digital Age

What an ordeal for curators to manage media and formats that keep going out of fashion but still come into the archive, each with different shapes, sizes, storage, and environmental requirements! The consequence, as we know too well, is that nonstandard materials tend to get

Figure 7.2. Recording Media[1]

	M/O/S*	A/D**	What to Know	Preservation Issues
Reel-to-Reel	M	A	Commonly used 1940s–1960s Sturdier than audiocassette Difficult to purchase	Tape approaching end of life Playback equipment hard to find Obsolescent Consider digitizing
Audiocassette	M	A	Most popular format for oral historians 1960s–2000 Most oral histories in archives on audiocassette	Lifespan 10–30 years, many are approaching end of life Lifespan dependent upon physical care, manufacturer Not a preservation format Consider digitizing
MiniDisc	O	D	Superceded by other digital formats Popular format early 2000s Cannot make direct digital copies	Lifespan unknown Easy to handle, shelve Obsolescent Not a preservation medium
DAT	M	D	Popular 1980s Format discontinued 2005 Excellent for recording	Obsolescent Not a preservation medium
Compact Disc[2] storage	O	D	Possible standard Convenient size and shape for archives Inexpensive	Possible standard for digital Durable Lifespan unknown, dependent on manufacturer, kind of CD
DVD	O	D	Holds more information than CD Popular for multimedia	Lifespan unknown Preservation qualities unknown Less stable than CD
Flash Card	S	D	Common in field recorders Excellent for recording	Expensive Lifespan unknown Not a preservation medium

Other formats – wax cylinder, wire recording, microcassettes, etc., are rare and non-standard. Archivists should work with experts to transfer to standard formats.

---

* Magnetic/Optical/Solid State   **Analog/Digital

---

1 Much information about recording media is conflicting or subject to rapid change. This table was compiled from a variety of sources, with an eye for highlighting the qualities most important for preservation and for representing the most general consensus.

2 However, in January 2006, computer storage expert Kurt Gerecke reported that *burned* CDs, as opposed to *pressed* CDs, have an expected lifespan of only 2 to 5 years, shattering hopes for CD becoming a preservation format. This report was widely discussed in the media, for example, in "Do burned CDs have a short life span?" by John Blau, *PC World*, (January 10, 2006).

ignored in the archive. This negligence factor further contributes to their vulnerability, since they get shifted to the problem shelf and continue to deteriorate, as confused archivists search for answers.

Preservation specialists acknowledge the problems that multiple formats cause curators. We all know we could manage our collections better if all the media lined up nicely on the shelf and had the same environmental requirements.

This is where digitization comes in. Recordings that have been digitized can be

- stored on media with the same size, shape, and environmental needs;
- **refreshed** and **reformatted** as a batch, from digital files stored on a server;
- used to make additional copies without loss of quality;
- played back on standard equipment, or on a computer;
- easily manipulated for editing, cleaning up, or combining with other media.

But digitization requires a whole new way of thinking about managing collections. Here are some of the concepts that archivists must address as we move into a digital environment.

BORN DIGITAL. More and more often, oral histories arrive in the archive **born digital**. Archivists must ensure they are accompanied by appropriate metadata, that file formats and versions are compatible with the archives equipment, and that digital files are virus free.

MEDIA-INDEPENDENT FILES. As the name implies, **media-independent** files are digital sound or video files that may arrive in the archive via email, FTP, or other data transfer—that is, not on anything you can pick up and hold on to. Managing documents without a physical carrier is a new concept for archivists, who must now pay attention to file formats, make decisions about copying onto physical media, and provide for user access.

SEPARATION OF CONTENT FROM CARRIER. In a traditional archive, we almost always thought of an item's content and its carrier as one in the same. Whether it is a paper document, an audiocassette, or an artifact, we considered the meaning inherent in the physical object. Not so in a digital world. The capability to transfer or reformat the content from one physical carrier or format to another, not only makes it possible to separate the content from its carrier, but is necessary to do so. As new technologies emerge and old ones become obsolete, curators must include the procedures for regularly refreshing and reformatting data.

METADATA. A key component to managing a digital archive is **metadata.** Literally, data

---

Figure 7.3 Terminology Note: Manipulating Digital Data

Digitize. To convert analog data (continuous signal) to binary electronic format.

Migrate. To move analog or digital data from one computer storage system to another.

Refresh. To make an exact copy of data to a newer medium of the same kind (e.g., from an old cassette to a new one) for preservation.

Reformat. To make a copy with a structure or format different from the original, in order to preserve the content.

about data, metadata can include a description of the content, information about the file itself, rights management information, and other information the institution wishes to record. Its purpose is to help computer systems interpret the digital file as it travels from one institutional server to another, to a library catalog, or to a website. Metadata is an essential component in the effective management of digital collections. Unfortunately, there are currently no metadata standards for oral histories.

We are living in a digital age; that is a fact. How we, as interviewers, curators, archivists, and program managers respond to it determines the effectiveness—as well as the long-term safety—of our collections. Elizabeth Cohen leaves no room for doubt, "Digitization forces a paradigm change. Librarians are used to thinking that copies are not the real things. The cult of the original is powerful in the world of analog recording, where information was lost with each generation. Today, however, the original digital material may be preserved in its pristine form anywhere and everywhere."[5]

PUTTING THEORY INTO PRACTICE

We practice preservation naturally when we lock the doors of the archive at the end of the day, print transcripts on acid-free paper, or make copies of recorded interviews. Much of preservation is based on common sense, and we practice it almost without thinking. However, a more comprehensive approach is *essential* for preserving our healthy documents into the long-term future, as well as rescuing our older collections from chemical deterioration and media obsolescence.

One way to approach this complicated issue is to develop a three-tiered plan. The first tier involves common sense and the application of the four principles mentioned earlier in this chapter. This can be accomplished easily through staff awareness. The next tier deals with preserving healthy documents into the future. This involves a written set of standards and procedures for the archive. It can usually be accomplished by existing staff, if time and funds are available. The third tier involves rescuing older materials that are already endangered. This level is complex, expensive, and almost always involves special expertise.

This section will help you get started thinking about preservation for your own oral history collection. It includes a section on evaluating the preservation needs of the collection, developing a plan, and exploring digitization. Be sure to refer to the sample forms in Appendix B, and the Resources section (Appendix D) for up-to-date information on current preservation practices.[6]

Evaluate

COLLECTION-LEVEL EVALUATION. The first step in developing a preservation plan is to evaluate the overall collection for its preservation needs. This should include an inventory of the physical items and an assessment of the environmental conditions where materials are stored. Use or adapt the *Collection Evaluation for Preservation* worksheet in Appendix B to collect this information.

If the collection is large or contains interviews on a variety of media, divide it into sections and evaluate each section separately. Make a note of any obvious problems, such as missing information on labels, or severely damaged media. The information you've collected on the worksheet will give you a snapshot of the overall condition of the collection and its environment. This will help you set priorities, decide whether to do an item-level evaluation, and determine what kinds of expertise are required for a preservation plan.

ITEM-LEVEL EVALUATION. If the collection is old or otherwise endangered, at some point you need to examine and evaluate the condition of every item. This is a time-consuming and costly process that usually involves preservation experts, but it is necessary in order to get an honest assessment of the collection. Sometimes it is required to get funding. Many curators take this opportunity to do a complete inventory, verify that cataloging is done and legal papers are in order, and enter data into a collection management system. Use or adapt the *Item-Level Evaluation for Preservation* in Appendix B for this task.[7]

Plan

Preservation cannot be done once and forgotten. Our collections need ongoing attention as older documents age and new ones are added, so that they will be sustainable into the indefinite future. Remember, many of our potential users are not yet born! Use or adapt the *Preservation Planning Checklist* in Appendix B and the comments below to guide your thinking and develop your own plan.

GOALS. Think about specific goals for preservation. Why are you undertaking this now? Have some media deteriorated to the point that preservation work must be done immediately? Is the preservation project part of a larger, multi-institutional effort? Are you developing a plan for a newly acquired collection or a new storage facility? Consider short-term, mid-term, and long-term goals.

WORKFLOW. Map out the practicalities of what, when, where, why, and by whom the preservation work will be done. Include the following:

- physical space needed for preservation work
- physical space needed for storing documents
- standards to be used for format transfer
- standards to be used for metadata
- procedures for documenting the work done
- additional tasks to be done, such as transcribing or cataloging
- deadline for completion

OUTCOMES. How many cassettes will be digitized? How many copies will be made and how will they be distributed? What reports or documentation will be produced? What additional access will be created through digitization? Translate goals into specific outcomes.

RESOURCES. Make a list of all the resources required to accomplish your goals—human, financial, and technical. Beside each category make notes about how your needs can be met. Do staff or volunteers have special skills that are underutilized? Can community organizations or another department on campus be tapped for recording equipment, or technical expertise? How about local grants or regional programs to create a digital archive? Think creatively and be sure to plan for the long-term as well as the short-term.

MAINTENANCE. Maintenance can be the most vulnerable of all preservation tasks. Staff come and go, institutional policies change, and preservation standards are rapidly evolving, but collection maintenance must be practiced on a regular basis over time. Be sure to add this item to your operational budget and develop clear written procedures that can be followed throughout staff transitions.

Digitize

Digitization has many advantages as a preservation tool, and is unquestionably the wave of the future. It helps protect original analog recordings from unnecessary handling, makes future preservation easier, and makes posting on the World Wide Web a possibility. Copies can be made from digital files without loss of quality. As the technology improves, this alternative will become even easier and more cost effective, helping us to preserve and provide better access to our oral history collections.[8]

WHEN TO CONSULT AN EXPERT

Any major preservation project requires team-work and expertise. Seek expert help if

- you know you have oral histories on media that are approaching the end of their life;
- you have oral histories with significant content but are not sure of their condition;
- you are ready to do a major collection evaluation;
- you are ready to do a major digitization project; or
- your preservation needs include film or video.

THE BOTTOM LINE

- Make copies of original recordings, and store them separately. Always keep the original.

- Distribution is a preservation principle. Put copies in multiple locations.
- Transcription is a preservation principle. A transcript preserves the *content* of the interview.
- Evaluate your collection, then prioritize. Recordings on deteriorated media are lost forever.
- Digitizing oral history collections has many advantages, but it is not essential—at least, not at the moment.

Useful Forms in Appendix B

Collection Evaluation for Preservation

Item-Level Evaluation for Preservation

Preservation Planning Checklist

CHAPTER 8

ORAL HISTORIES ON THE INTERNET

Everything should be made as simple as possible, but not one bit simpler.

—Albert Einstein

The Internet is quickly becoming the most popular and the best way for oral historians to reach their audience. In many ways this new delivery method is perfectly suited to our work.

- It reaches a *global audience.* Anyone with an Internet connection can access oral histories that are physically located in even the remotest corner of the world.

- It offers *precision retrieval.* Not only can users find an interview on the World Wide Web, but they can also zero in on specific topics within an interview.

- *Multimedia* makes it possible to listen, read, or view an interview, or even to listen/view and read at the same time. It is a platform for online exhibitions that guide users from one document to another, or one medium to another, to get a rich and varied introduction to a topic.

- *Hyperlinks* connect related topics within a web page, or from one website to another. Users can customize information gathering by following hyperlinks to hone in on a topic, without scanning a recording or transcript sequentially.

- *Online access privileges* can be designed to protect narrators' privacy. Privileges can be designed in tiers, to give different user communities the level of access they need, and to block unauthorized users.

The wonder of the Internet is both a gift and a challenge to information providers. It forces us, as oral historians, project managers, and curators, to rethink almost every aspect of our jobs. With this rapidly evolving frontier upon us, we should assume that at some point in the near future our collections will be available on the World Wide Web, and we must keep this in mind in all our planning.

In spite of the technology, curators are slow to replicate oral history collections online, and those of us who have done so are grappling with technical, legal, and administrative questions. As I was surveying oral history websites for this book, over and over I came upon URLs that had disappeared, broken links, websites that couldn't be navigated, or announcements for exciting features that didn't exist.

We can excuse ourselves for fumbling when we remember how quickly this trajectory is moving. In the year 2000 University of

---

Figure 8.1. World Wide Web vs. Internet

The World Wide Web is a part of the Internet that is made up of websites accessible via a **browser,** such as Explorer or Firefox.

The Internet is a vast computer network for data exchange, which includes the World Wide Web, email, FTP, instant messaging, and other protocols.

Since so much Internet use is via the World Wide Web, the terms are often used interchangeably.

Alaska-Fairbanks research associate Karen Brewster conducted a survey of oral history projects online.[1] She found and reviewed sixty-four oral history programs that had a presence on the World Wide Web. At this time, fewer than half posted any content, and most of those were excerpts of oral histories, not the full interview. The remainder offered a list, finding aid, or just a description of the program.

My own 2004 survey[2] asked about how we currently use the World Wide Web for our collections, and also about our hopes and dreams for the future. Twenty of the sixty-two respondents had no online presence at all. More than half had an institutional website, but no online access to their collections. Of the remaining, twenty-seven reported summaries, finding aids, or some form of excerpts (text or audio). Only one respondent reported a complete digital archive of video and transcripts, available to registered visitors.

Most of us are excited, confused, and overwhelmed by the possibilities of the Internet, but we have a long way to go before we fully realize our dreams.

THE BIG QUESTIONS

Though most curators and oral historians understand the importance of the Internet for providing access to collections, the practical issues—technical, legal, financial, and logistical—force us to proceed slowly. This is not so bad, since best practices for oral histories on the Internet are still being ironed out. Here are some of the big questions.

The Website

How shall we present our collections on a website to best meet our users' needs? Post excerpts or the complete document? Audio/visual, or transcript, or both? Replicate the physical archive? Use multimedia and hyperlinks to add context?

Narrators' Rights

How does privacy on the Internet differ from privacy in a physical archive? Who is responsible for protecting these rights? Where does one draw the line between protecting privacy and limiting access?

Legal and Ethical Issues

Are pre-Internet legal consent forms adequate for Internet distribution? If so, do curators have an ethical responsibility to contact narrators before posting on the Internet? What does *informed* consent mean in an Internet environment if we have no control over how, or by whom, interviews will be used (or abused)?

Website Development and Maintenance

What is the goal in developing an online presence, and how can it best be accomplished?

Figure 8.2. Permanency on the World Wide Web

A *website* is simply an interface between the information and the user. It determines what users see and how it is arranged. A website can disappear forever, or the content can change without notice. Unless determined otherwise, a website should never be considered a permanent resource.

A *digital archive*, on the other hand, is a true archive in digital format, which is often (though not always) available via the World Wide Web. Users can trust that a digital archive will be managed according to archival standards for digital formats, and that the content is permanent.

What hardware and software are needed? What technical expertise is required and how can we meet these needs? What are the pros and cons of incorporating multimedia? Who will maintain the website once it is up and running?

Cost

Who will pay the stupendous cost of developing and maintaining a comprehensive website: initial design; domain and licensing; digitizing materials; rights management; coding, formatting and programming; server space; and ongoing maintenance?

EXAMPLES FROM REAL LIFE

Some oral history programs have answered these questions successfully, and have developed creative solutions to accomplish their objectives using the World Wide Web. Here are examples of four effective, but very different, approaches.

Denshō: The Japanese American Legacy Project

http://www.densho.org/. Denshō uses digital technology to preserve and make accessible primary source materials on the incarceration of Japanese Americans during World War II. Founded in 1997 by two information technology executives, the project has the financial resources and the technical expertise to provide a comprehensive knowledge base on this topic. Access to Denshō is online only; there is no physical archive.

Denshō's collection consists of 240 **born digital**, **visual histories** (more than 450 hours of video footage), supplemented by photographs, maps, and related documents. The project's goal is to make the entire collection available online, but at the same time to protect narrators' testimonies against misuse. To accomplish this, Denshō staff designed a website with two primary sections: the publicly accessible section and the registration-only full archive. The public website has general-interest modules and teaching tools. The restricted section, which contains the complete archive of visual histories and their transcripts, is available only to registered users who agree to abide by Denshō's legally binding *Terms of Use*. The registration process can be completed online; but each application is examined by a staff member.

Best use of technology has always been a priority for Denshō. The importance of achieving a balance between the technology and the overall mission is the ultimate goal. Technical Manager Geoff Froh says, "Technology can introduce unnecessary complexity into an organization. There are real costs to supporting a highly technology-reliant infrastructure, from the purchase of the equipment to long-term maintenance and upgrades. Though systems administration can consume a great deal of staff time, we cannot let technology divert our organizational focus. The drive to develop a sophisticated data model or deploy a 'cool' website can crowd out the underlying purpose of the project. We are about people telling their stories. Information technology facilitates that work; it is not an end in itself."[3]

Maria Rogers Oral History Program

http://www.bplcarnegie.org/oralhistory. The Maria Rogers Oral History Program has been collecting and archiving oral histories which document life in the city and county of Boulder, Colorado, since 1976. This community-based program is supported by the Boulder Public Library, an endowment, a strong volunteer base, and an energetic program manager.

Even though oral histories are available at Boulder's Carnegie Branch Library for Local History, program administrators want to use the Internet to make the collection as widely available as possible. With this in mind, they digitized their 900 analog audio interviews, and since then have recorded 500 additional interviews in digital video. Currently, the entire collection of more than 1,400 audio and visual interviews, along with transcripts and/or summaries, is available online at the MROHP digital archive. The excellently designed website provides an alphabetical and numerical index of narrators, technical tips for users, instructions for copyright and permission to use, and guidelines for finding information by topic. Names and topics can also be retrieved using the library's online catalog and Google.

While preparing pre-Internet interviews for online access, staff members pondered the legal right to do so. Program Manager Susan Becker explains, "Our attorney told us our permission form was sufficient for legally posting interviews to the Internet. However, ethically we felt we should make a good faith effort to locate interviewees and request their permission. We sent hundreds of letters to past interviewees. . . . If we did not hear back . . . we still posted that interview on our website, but will take it down if anyone [contacts us and asks us to]."[4] (Permission letter is reproduced in Appendix B.)

Project Jukebox, University of Alaska, Fairbanks

www.uaf.edu/library/jukebox. Project Jukebox is probably the first large oral history project to use digital technology for preservation and access. Currently thirty online exhibitions, called jukeboxes, showcase an array of Alaskan and Polar topics by weaving audio, text, photos, and maps into self-contained multimedia programs.

The jukebox idea began as a digital preservation project in 1988 with a start-up grant from Apple Computer and the creative thinking born of a project fighting for survival.[5] Interviews from the university's oral history collection were digitized and developed into interactive multimedia CD-ROMs around a

particular region, community, or topic. Ever mindful of their remote location, this Fairbanks-based project wanted to reach a dual audience—the rural Alaskan communities who are subjects of the jukeboxes, and interested users around the world. The Internet is the obvious solution, and in 2000 the first jukebox came online.

Legal, ethical, and cultural concerns underpin this project. According to Program Director William Schneider, "Native peoples are tired of being studied by outsiders. Jukeboxes address this concern and give future researchers a broad base to compare different accounts. The potential to create historical dialogue between academics and community based members is immense. . . . We know we are headed in the right direction, but the technical challenges and ethical issues . . . are daunting."[6] The site-use agreement (reproduced in Appendix B), which pops up before entering a jukebox, stipulates not only requirements for re-use, but also that materials be used with proper respect.

Regional Oral History Office (ROHO), University of California, Berkeley

http://bancroft.berkeley.edu/ROHO/. ROHO has been building its oral history collection since 1954 and has one of the oldest and largest oral history archives in the country. The collection includes more than two thousand oral histories related to the San Francisco Bay Area, the West, and the United States. More than one hundred new oral histories are added annually.

ROHO's collections are widely accessible even without the Internet. The office is physically located at the University of California-Berkeley, in the San Francisco Bay Area, and collections are available to the public at the Bancroft Library on the university campus. ROHO transcripts are also available for purchase, and libraries around the world have added selected oral histories to their own collections.

Though the ROHO website provides access to its collections, the most effective access is through the **EAD** encoded transcripts in the Online Archive of California (OAC) (http://www.oac.cdlib.org/). The OAC is a digital archive that provides access to California's online collections through a single search engine. ROHO's oral histories benefit on two counts: The *depth* of access to each oral history is increased through the ability to browse the Table of Contents and navigate directly to a topic, as well as to search for keywords within a transcript. The *breadth* of access is increased since users can do a single search across OAC's database, and get results from other institutions to supplement the oral history material they are interested in.

ROHO's challenge for the near future is the enormous task of converting an institutional lifetime's work into a format that can be used by OAC. Digitization and EAD encoding are both expensive and labor intensive. Associate Director Vic Geraci warns of the time and resources required for such an effort. In the meantime, he says, "ROHO is pleased to make full transcripts available on the ROHO website."[7]

PLANNING FOR AN INTERNET PRESENCE: WHAT CURATORS NEED TO KNOW

If your project isn't online yet, you aren't alone, and you have the advantage of learning from the experience of others.[8] If you do have an online presence, you've probably discovered that creating and maintaining a website cannot just be tacked on to the duties of existing staff, to be done in their spare time. It is a demanding task that requires special skills and thoughtful design, expertise and patience, a plan for ongoing content management, and resources for software and hardware purchase and upgrades.

It is impossible to develop an effective website without teamwork. Technical experts can provide the structure and form for the website, and oral historians or curators provide the content. In addition, team members should include institutional administrators to make decisions about fund allocation, licensing, and partnerships; legal experts to review and approve the fuzzy legal issues; sound engineers to digitize recordings; and other staff to scan documents, manage the database, and create metadata.

It sounds like a huge undertaking, and it is. On one hand, it may be wise to wait for the right moment—the long-awaited grant, the best experts to form the web-team, and the best technology options. However, most of us know the day will never come when all factors line up. We want to plunge in, take risks, do the best we can, and be proud of our work.

In either case, start planning by addressing these questions:

Goals

Be specific. Do you want to replicate your physical archive online? Post selected high profile oral histories? Promote an event or special project? Create an educational tool? Create an online exhibition?

Audience

Who will be most interested in your website? Local users who will eventually visit the physical archive? Remote users whom you will never see? What is their technology level? What is their educational level?

Medium

Will you post transcript, audio, video, or all three? Summaries, excerpts, or complete document? Will you provide the opportunity for users' feedback?

Figure 8.3. Internet Access to Oral Histories: Understanding the Options

OPTIONS	PROS	CONS
Library online catalog	Online presence No extra work if you are connected to a library, happens automatically with cataloging	Limited access. Catalog record points to physical item in library, oral histories themselves not online Currently not available through Google
Finding aid or summary	Easy to post Fewer issues with narrator's privacy Directs universal audience to physical archive	Limited access. Finding aid points to physical item in library, oral histories themselves not online
Full transcript .pdf	Easiest way to post full transcript Can do word search within a document Protects document—users can't copy and paste text	Can't use hyperlinks to lead to related information Takes longer to load Large files require more storage
Full transcript .html	Hyperlinks direct users to related data or multimedia	Need technical expertise to encode transcript Users can copy and paste text
EAD encoded text	Better access to information within transcript Information can be exchanged from one database/website to another	Requires technical expertise
A/V recording—excerpts	User can hear or see narrator Returns the "oral" to oral history	Technical expertise required to manage sound files Large files require lots of storage space Some users not equipped for streaming audio
A/V recording—complete	Most authentic. Provides users with the full document from any remote location. Requires expertise to post and maintain	Large files require lots of storage space Users may not have computer capacity

Collection

Which interviews will you post, and why? Are interviews organized into series or other categories? Is there already a unifying topic(s) among interviews? Can you link oral histories by related content? Will photos, maps, or other documents supplement the interviews?

Rights Management

Are the legal issues resolved to the curator's satisfaction?

Preparation

Are recordings in digital format? Are transcripts in digital format? Is server space allocated for existing oral histories and for new interviews as they are conducted? Is metadata complete?

Certain features on a website, such as audio/video or a database, are more expensive than others. Weigh the cost of your dream website against how it will achieve your goals and benefit your primary audience. Also, factor in any limitations that are beyond your control: legal issues that can't be resolved, oral histories not yet digitized, limited administrative support, or lack of technical staff. A website is a big commitment for the present and for the future.

SOME OTHER OPTIONS

If you aren't ready to develop a website for your project, there are several other options for providing access to your collection on the Internet.

Library Connection

If your project is connected to a library, consider asking them to catalog oral histories. Catalog records would be available online through the library's **OPAC** (online catalog), and probably on the international library database **OCLC**'s WorldCat.

Online Archive

Some digital archives are built through contributions of materials from other institutions. They work much like a physical archive which accepts oral histories from individual or institutional researchers and incorporates them into the (usually subject-specific) archive. Each archive has specific requirements for contributions. Some examples are Online Archive of California (California Digital Library), Historical Voices (MATRIX, Michigan State University), and the Veterans History Project (Library of Congress).[9]

Commercial Database

Oral History Online (http://www.alexander street.com/products/orhi.htm) is a comprehensive database of oral histories, designed and operated by Alexander Street Press, a respected commercial content provider. This database is available through subscribing libraries around the world. Since all databases are enriched by high-quality content, Alexander Street Press encourages contributions from any oral history project that has content online in any form, including complete audio and video. A free companion database, *In the First Person* (http://www.inthefirstperson.com), is an index of personal documents, including 17,000 oral histories.

THE BOTTOM LINE

The importance of the World Wide Web will only grow as a medium for information delivery. Oral historians, archivists, and project managers are experimenting with various models for how to best use this powerful resource, and best practices will surely emerge in the next few years for presenting oral histories online. Keep these points in mind as your plan for your own online presence.

- The World Wide Web is the best way to reach a broad and diverse audience, but is also expensive and technically demanding.

- When you plan your website, budget for ongoing content management and maintenance, as well as the initial designs.

- Make sure legal issues are resolved to the satisfaction of institutional administrators.

- Make sure your plans further the two goals of archives: access and preservation.

Useful Forms in Appendix B

Retrospective Consent to Publish on the Internet

Online Site Use Agreement

CHALLENGES OF THE 21ST CENTURY

> In a time of drastic change it is the learners who inherit the future. The learned usually find themselves equipped to live in a world that no longer exists.
>
> —Eric Hoffer

Eric Hoffer's words got me thinking about the importance of connecting the past to the present, and the present to the future. As archivists, we are reminded of this every day, when we fill research requests for documents that were created in the past. Researchers use primary documents—photographs, menus and flyers, diaries and letters, and of course, oral histories—to piece together a picture of how life was lived in another time and place—what people dreamed and complained and laughed about, what songs they sang, and what stories they told their children.

Our role in connecting to the future is less obvious but every bit as important, as we process contemporary documents or rescue older ones for the benefit of future users. A new generation of researchers is beginning to find its way to the archives, alongside traditional scholars, and oral histories are frequently on their request list. Educators, website designers, filmmakers, artists, and museum curators—the users of the future—bring new expectations and make new demands on our collections. They are interested not only in the content of oral histories, but also in the voices and visual images—in broadcast quality—so they can reproduce them in their own creative work.

Tragically, we cannot always fill their requests, even when we have the documents in the archive. Perhaps the recording medium has deteriorated too much to be played, or the sound quality is too poor. Or maybe we just can't find the recording in the vault. Worse still, the recorded interview may be available and in good condition, but can't be released because the legal permissions are missing. These predicaments, unfortunately, are common occurrences in archives.

But we can hardly be blamed. If ever there was a time of drastic change for oral historians, archivists, and curators, it is now. Our jobs are impacted on three fronts: We must hasten to rescue the older recordings on deteriorating media, especially audiocassettes; we must keep abreast of the technology learning curve for managing digital collections; and we must meet our new user needs.

Here are some examples of issues which confound curators of oral histories today.

Collections

Archivists and oral historians acknowledge the communication gap between their worlds. When archivists don't know the oral historian's intention and oral historians don't understand how to prepare materials for an archive, the oral history suffers, as does the historical record. Currently, there are neither standard guidelines for unaffiliated oral historians to prepare their oral histories for archives, nor for archives to evaluate an oral history collection for acquisition.

User Expectations

As collections grow in size and visibility, so do demands for their use. Not only do users who come into the archive expect high-quality sound, video, and full-text transcript, but potential users around the world expect the same, from their home computers. Curators struggle to meet new user expectations, along with new protocols for cataloging/metadata, online access, permission to use, and the technology that accompanies it. There are many questions and few answers.

Technology

Traditionally, archivists have performed their job well without getting too involved in technology. This is no longer the case. At the very least, archivists and curators must understand the technology involved in recording, cataloging, project management, preservation, and access. In smaller archives, they might be completely responsible for these functions. The learning curve is steep, and guidance for applying technology to curating oral histories is scarce.

Rights Management

Information providers are actively discussing whether the protocols for permission to use, informed consent, and interviewer privacy are the same or different as the access to collections shifts from a physical archive to an online environment. What does it mean to the archive and to the narrator if interviews are available to anyone anywhere in the world? Are there more opportunities for misuse or abuse? What is lost if there is no personal relationship between the archivist and the user? How do we find out about an infringement, and who is responsible if this happens? Curators are struggling to strike a balance between open access to collections and protecting the narrator's privacy.

❖

Five national-level surveys[1] support the findings of my own research as testimony that our cultural heritage is at risk, and that oral histories are high on the endangered list. Though curating oral histories will always be problematic, I believe a great deal can be done to streamline the process from interview to archive, through standards, best practices, and increased communication between oral historians and archivists.

Initiatives should be undertaken at high levels to create protocols that are sustainable, scalable, inclusive, and affordable. In fact, if steps are not taken soon, the rich cultural heritage embedded in our oral histories may be lost forever.

Here are some suggestions for working toward this goal:

- Establish a clearinghouse for small or unaffiliated oral history projects to connect to appropriate repositories.

- Establish guidelines for oral historians to prepare recorded interviews for the archive.

- Establish guidelines for archives to evaluate an oral history collection for acquisition.

- Include archival principles in oral history education.

- Develop a simple and scalable model for processing oral histories, in order to keep costs low, and to avoid backlogs.

- Establish an Interview-to-Archive toolkit with templates, checklists, technology tips, and simple instructions for practitioners at any level.

- Maintain a website for technical information as it applies to curating oral histories, including a users forum for sharing personal experiences.

- Partner with a software firm to develop an affordable project management database for curating oral histories.

- Develop standards and best practices pertaining specifically to oral histories
  - for legal and ethical issues in the Digital Age
  - for cataloging and metadata
  - for preservation of recording and content
  - for presentation on the World Wide Web.
- Participate actively in large, collaborative projects for preserving recorded materials and for incorporating oral histories into digital archives.

Our job as curator is both art and science. The Digital Age offers us new opportunities, and it forces us to question time-tested practices and standards. As we move forward we must find the balance between innovation and tradition. It is our task and our privilege to usher the past, in the form of the human voice, into the future.

NOTES

Preface

[1] I posted a request to complete the survey on five professional lists: H-Oralhist, Archives, Autocat, H-Public, and H-Museum. A copy of the survey, analysis of the results, and list of respondents is posted at http://www.nancymackay.net/curating.

Introduction

[1] The survey and results are posted at http://www.nancymackay.net/curating.

Chapter One

[1] "The expanding role of the librarian in oral history," in David Dunaway and Willa K. Baum, *Oral history: an interdisciplinary anthology.* (Altamira Press, 1996). 321–340. Adapted from a 1976 lecture at the Louisiana State University Library School and originally published in *Library Lectures 6* (1978).

[2] Ibid. 322. The remaining Cs: creating, consuming, and counseling.

[3] Ibid. 326.

[4] Alessandro Portelli. *The Battle of Valle Giulia: oral history and the art of dialogue.* (University of Wisconsin Press, 1997). viii.

Chaper Two

[1] For description, see Chapter 6: Cataloging; for rights management, see Chapter 3: Legal & Ethical Issues; and for preservation, see Chapter 7: Preservation. Access is covered throughout the book. See the Resources section for references to general archival practice.

Chapter Three

[1] John Neuenschwander. *Oral history and the law.* 3rd ed. (Oral History Association, 2002). 5.

[2] Ibid. 6.

[3] If compensation is exchanged between two parties, the agreement falls under contract law. For more on contract law, see Neuenschwander, 32–33.

[4] Fair use issues are most common in academic institutions. University of Texas has an easy-to-understand fair use statement online at http://www.utsystem.edu/OGC/intellectualProperty/copypol2.htm

[5] One exception is a defamation suit filed against the Regional Oral History Office (ROHO) at University of California, Berkeley. The court ruled in ROHO's favor. See opinion at http://www.courtinfo.ca.gov/opinions/revpub/A106618.DOC

[6] *Handbook for oral history in the National Park Service.* http://www.cr.nps.gov/history/oh/oral.htm

[7] Society of American Archivists. *Code of Ethics.*

[8] Neuenschwander. 19–20. "The accepted rule is that anyone who repeats, republishes, or redistributes a defamatory statement made by another can be held liable as well. . . . Each individual or group that takes part in the publication of the defamatory words is chargeable as a primary publisher."

[9] Barbara W. Sommer and Mary Kay Quinlan. *Oral history manual.* (AltaMira Press, 2002). 19.

[10] William Schneider. *So they understand: cultural issues in oral history.* (Utah State University Press, 2002). 151–152.

[11] Geoff Froh. Email communication.

Chapter Four

[1] Two great places to start are Andy Kovolos' *Audio Field Recording Equipment Guide,* at the Vermont Folklife Center website, http://www.vermontfolklifecenter.org/res_audioequip.htm; and the Historical Voices section on oral history, http://www.historicalvoices.org/oralhistory/audio-tech.html. The Resources section in this book has a more comprehensive list.

Chapter Five

[1] Michael Frisch. "Oral history and the digital revolution: toward a post-documentary sensibility." In *The oral history reader.* 2nd ed., Robert Perks and Alistair Thomson, eds. (Routledge, 2006). First presented as a paper at the Roma International Oral History Association Conference, 2004.

[2] Ibid. This article is the most comprehensive analysis of audio indexing for oral histories.

Chapter Six

[1] In spite of time-tested cataloging standards, librarians are beginning the question the effectiveness of a traditional catalog in an era when users can go directly to the content. The Library of Congress commissioned a study, undertaken by Karen Calhoun of Cornell University, to examine this issue. The resulting report, *The changing nature of the catalog and its integration with other discovery tools* (March 2006), online at http://www.loc.gov/catdir/calhoun-report-final.pdf, is generating a great deal of discussion, and is sure to initiate changes in the next few years.

[2] An excellent introduction to the metadata is Murtha Baca's *Introduction to metadata: pathways to digital information*. Available in print from the Getty Research Center or online at http://www.getty.edu/research/conducting_research/standards/intrometadata/.

[3] http://authorities.loc.gov/. The Resources section (Appendix D) has examples of other controlled vocabularies.

Chapter Seven

[1] A follow-up conference, *Folk Heritage Collections in Crisis*, was held in December 2000. Conference proceedings are available online and in print at http://www.clir.org/pubs/reports/pub96/contents.html. Results of a third, more comprehensive study on the state of U.S. cultural collections were released in late 2005. This survey, undertaken by Heritage Preservation and the Institute of Museum and Library Services examined collections from a wide range of cultural institutions, from schools to public libraries to zoos. A summary of the results is available at the Heritage Preservation website, at http://www.heritage preservation.org/HHI.

[2] Abby Smith, David Randal Allen, and Karen Allen. *Survey of the state of audio collections in academic libraries*. (CLIR, 2004). Available online at http://www.clir.org/pubs/reports/pub128/contents.html. Participants included selected ARL (Association of Research Libraries) libraries, and Oberlin Group libraries (a consortium of seventy-five private, liberal arts colleges in the U.S.).

[3] Copies in analog formats, e.g., from one audiocassette to another, lose quality with each generation, so it is important to make one preservation master and all subsequent copies from it. In a digital environment, copies are theoretically clones of each other, so the distinction between original and copy is less significant; however, the principle of multiple copies is equally important.

[4] Elizabeth Cohen. "Preservation of audio." In *Folk heritage collections in crisis*. (CLIR, 2001). 20.

[5] Ibid. 21.

[6] The two best places to start are *CoOL (Conservation Online)* website, sponsored by Stanford University, http://palimpsest.stanford.edu/, and the Collaborative Digitization Program at http://www.cdpheritage.org. Both websites have a variety of tools for all levels of preservation needs and are frequently updated.

[7] An even more comprehensive evaluation tool has been developed by Mike Casey, at the Archives of Traditional Music at Indiana University. This tool, called FACET, uses a point system to evaluate and rank audio items based on the level of media deterioration and the overall risk. This tool helps curators prioritize collections by the level of risk, and to establish priorities for preservation by using metrics to come up with a "risk score" that factors in both the value of the content and the condition of the physical media it resides on. FACET is available on Indiana University's Sound Directions website, http://dlib.indiana.edu/projects/sounddirections/.

[8] An excellent document for getting started with digitization is *Digital audio best practices* (CDP Digital Audio Working Group, 2005), online at http://www.cdpheritage.org/digital/audio/documents/CDPDABP_1-2.pdf.

Chapter Eight

[1] Karen Brewster. *Internet access to oral recordings: finding the issues*. 2000. Online at http://www.uaf.edu/library/oralhistory/brewster1/. The appendix includes a list of the websites reviewed, along with Brewster's comments.

[2] Nancy MacKay. *Curating oral histories: survey results*. http://www.nancymackay.net/curating/finalSurveyResults.htm. My study surveyed any oral history project that archived their work, while Karen Brewster looked at only projects with an Internet presence.

[3] Response to author's questionnaire, February 20, 2005.

[4] Response to author's questionnaire, February 1, 2005.

[5] William Schneider. *So they understand: cultural issues in oral history*. (Utah State University Press, 2002). 28.

[6] Ibid.

[7] Telephone conversation with the author, April, 2006.

[8] An excellent place to start is Daniel Cohen & Roy Rosenzweig's *Digital history: a guide to gathering, preserving and presenting the past on the web.* (University of Pennsylvania, 2006), online at http://www.chnm.gmu.edu/digitalhistory/. As the title suggests, this work provides a comprehensive look at the issues involved with presenting history online, including website design for presenting history. Both authors are directors of the Center for New Media.

[9] Online Archive of California (California Digital Library), http://www.oac.cdlib.org/

Historical Voices (MATRIX), http://matrix.msu.edu/hist_voice.php

Veteran's History Project (Library of Congress), http://www.loc.gov/vets/

Chapter Nine

[1] *A public trust at risk: the heritage health index report on the state of America's collections.* 2003. http://www.heritagepreservation.org/HHI/full.html/. Survey of the health of U.S. collections in museums, historical societies, libraries, archives, historical societies, and scientific institutes.

A survey of Digital Cultural Heritage Initiatives (DCHIs) and their sustainability concerns. 2002. http://www.clir.org/pubs/abstract/pub118abst.html. Survey of thirty-three North American DCHIs examining scope, financing, organizational structure and sustainability potential.

Survey of the state of audio collections in academic libraries. 2003. http://www.clir.org/pubs/reports/pub128/pub128.pdf.

Survey of folk heritage collections. 2000. http://www.clir.org/pubs/reports/pub96/appendix2.html. Survey of U.S. ethnographic audio collections.

Where history begins, a report on historical records repositories in the United States. 1998. http://www.statearchivists.org/reports/HRRS/HRRSALL.PDF. Assessment of existing collections and their greatest needs.

APPENDIX A
PROFILES OF ORAL HISTORY PROGRAMS

This section profiles the seven oral history programs that participated as case studies for this book.

CENTER FOR ORAL AND PUBLIC HISTORY, California State University, Fullerton, a university-sponsored oral history program since 1968.

DENSHŌ DIGITAL ARCHIVE, a nonprofit, digital-only archive devoted to recording and preserving the testimonies of Japanese Americans who were incarcerated during World War II.

IDAHO ORAL HISTORY CENTER, a program within a state historical society, devoted to collecting and preserving the oral histories of Idaho residents.

MARIA ROGERS ORAL HISTORY PROGRAM, an oral history program within a public library, devoted to collecting, archiving, and providing access to oral histories on all aspects of Boulder County, Colorado.

THE ORAL HISTORY PROJECT (VIETNAM ARCHIVE), a separately funded program located within a major state university, devoted to collecting and preserving the history of the Vietnam War through oral history.

UAF ORAL HISTORY PROGRAM, an oral history program and archive within a university library, devoted to collecting, preserving, and providing access to recorded interviews of Alaskan interest.

VETERANS' ORAL HISTORY PROJECT, a project within a public library, devoted to recording and preserving the life stories of men and women veterans living in and around Natick, Massachusetts.

CENTER FOR ORAL AND PUBLIC HISTORY

California State University
Fullerton, California
http://coph.fullerton.edu/

MISSION/GOALS To document Orange County and the surrounding area through oral history and public history projects.

AGE Since 1968, but with changes over the years. In 2003, the program became COPH, a nationally recognized center for oral and public history.

INSTITUTION Oral history program within a major state university

FUNDING University provides funds (as faculty release time) for administrators. Collections Curator and Systems Librarian positions supported through soft money. Income generated through transcribing and binding service, workshops, and fees for copies, etc. Grants secured for special projects, such as digitization.

STAFF Collection Curator (.5 FTE) manages the project—both incoming interviews and retrospective processing. Director, Associate Director, Systems Librarian have additional responsibilities outside COPH. Graduate students, interns, and volunteers complete staff needs.

COLLECTION More than 4,000 audio interviews: 2,200 recorded on open-reel tape (currently being digitized) and 1,200 on audiocassette. Most interviews generated by CSUF class projects, coordinated by Collection Curator.

PHYSICAL SPACE Located in university library, though not officially affiliated. All materials stored in 1,200-square-foot archive. Curator's office and reading room.

INTERVIEWS Most interviews conducted by CSUF students as part of coursework and for M.A. theses and projects. Collection Curator trains student interviewers and provides procedures for delivering completed interviews to archive. 150–200 interviews added per year.

TRANSCRIPTS More than half the interviews have been transcribed. Currently considering foregoing this step as digital technologies improve access.

CATALOG Not catalogued at this time; basic information entered into a spreadsheet.

PRESERVATION All tapes are digitized. Preservation master and user copies made on CD.

ACCESS Website considered most important point of access. Oral histories can be found through Google.

SECRETS TO SUCCESS Student generated oral histories make it easy to build a diverse and growing collection. Dedicated and knowledgeable staff. Location within CSUF facilitates access and walk-in traffic. Income-generating services.

CHALLENGES Processing current oral histories as well as backlog. Rescuing older tapes. Keeping records and reconstructing data for older oral histories.

DENSHŌ DIGITAL ARCHIVE

Denshō: The Japanese American Legacy Project
Seattle, Washington
http://www.densho.org/

MISSION/GOALS	To preserve the testimonies of Japanese Americans who were unjustly incarcerated during World War II. These firsthand accounts, coupled with historical images and teacher resources, explore the principles of democracy and equal justice.
AGE	Since 1997.
INSTITUTION	Independent, nonprofit organization.
FUNDING	Most funding comes from private donors and fundraising events. Additional funds from government and private foundation grants.
STAFF	4.5 full-time staff; professionals in subject area, technology, fundraising, and community outreach.
COLLECTION	About 250 visual histories (over 540 hours filmed), and growing. A few additional donated oral histories. Conduct 15–20 in-depth interviews per year.
PHYSICAL SPACE	Since this is a digital archive, physical space is for staff, servers, production, and processing. Master videotapes stored in offsite storage facilities.
INTERVIEWS	Currently conducted by staff members. Interviewers highly trained and carefully matched to narrator.
TRANSCRIPTS	Interviews transcribed in-house and by commercial service. Transcripts are audit-checked, then sent to narrator for final review.
CATALOG	Traditional cataloging not done, but principles of authority control, indexing, and description incorporated into metadata plan.
PRESERVATION	Preservation is a high priority and Denshō is planning for the future. Preservation master copies and originals are stored offsite. Plan in place for format refreshment.
ACCESS	All access through website. Tiered system whereby general educational material is available to drop-by website visitors, but full visual histories are available only through prior registration.
SECRETS TO SUCCESS	Denshō focuses on rigorous oral history methodology and deep engagement with the community. The staff is an integrated team of forward-thinking, flexible professionals.
CHALLENGES	Preserving stories before they disappear. Providing useful access to a growing archive. Connecting work to current themes.

IDAHO ORAL HISTORY CENTER

Idaho State Historical Society Library and Archives
Boise, Idaho
http://www.idahohistory.net/

MISSION/GOALS	Collects oral histories of Idahoans who have lived through Idaho's history. Topics include frontier and pioneer life, Civilian Conservation Corps, Women's Movement, and various ethnic groups.
AGE	Since 1989.
INSTITUTION	Program within historical society.
FUNDING	Dedicated funds from ISHS, and from Oral History Center through the sale of *A Field Notebook for Oral History*, and copies of recordings.
STAFF	Staff oral historian (1.0 FTE) does project design, interviews, processing, and community outreach. Office assistant (.5 FTE) does transcribing and office tasks.
COLLECTION	3,000 interviews and growing. Add about 200 interviews per year as funds and time allow. Most interviews taped on analog audio, although more recent interviews conducted with digital recording equipment.
PHYSICAL SPACE	Oral History Center located within the Idaho History Center (IHC). Shared space includes a staff area and audio-visual room. Master copies of recordings and transcripts are located in two separate rooms inside IHC; public copies of recordings and transcripts are located within IHC's research library.
INTERVIEWS	Approximately two-thirds of interviews were done either before IOHC was officially created, or by outside persons and donated to IOHC. Remaining interviews conducted by staff oral historian, interns, and volunteers.
TRANSCRIPTS	Interviews are transcribed when time and funds allow, by Center office assistant, interns, and volunteers.
CATALOG	Catalogued into collection management system, which converts data to a MARC record. These records are sent to NUCMC[1] where catalogers clean up record, initiate authority control, and load onto NUCMC's union catalog and RLIN.[2]
PRESERVATION	No official preservation plan. Rewind or copy cassettes when a request is made.
ACCESS	Website (list and summaries), in-house catalog, and NUCMC catalog. Honor requests to send copies of tapes for a fee.
SECRETS TO SUCCESS	Since its inception in 1978, there has always been an oral historian, office staff, interns, and volunteers. This dedication has helped to overcome the challenges. The IOHC has always had strong support from ISHS administration, which has helped it continue through some hard financial times.
CHALLENGES	To maintain the IOHC's goals: gather, preserve, and provide access to oral histories, and educate Idahoans (and whoever else will listen) about oral history and our oral history projects—while working with a limited staff and budget. In the 21st century, the new challenge is to migrate the super-majority of our collection from analog to digital.

[1] National Union Catalog of Manuscript Collections (Library of Congress)
[2] **Bibliographic Utility**.

MARIA ROGERS ORAL HISTORY PROGRAM

Carnegie Branch Library for Local History, Boulder Public Library
Boulder, Colorado
http://www.bplcarnegie.org/oralhistory

MISSION/GOALS	Collects, archives, and makes available to the public oral histories on all aspects of life in Boulder County, Colorado.
AGE	Since 1976, but has grown and changed dramatically, especially since 1997.
INSTITUTION	Oral history program within public library.
FUNDING	Management funded by an endowment. Other staffing, technical support, supplies, and physical space provided by Boulder Public Library. Funding for special projects and equipment provided by grants.
STAFF	Program manager, .5 FTE; additional hours funded from time to time by grants. Technical support and cataloger are BPL staff. Thirty active volunteers are interviewers, transcribers, archivists, and videographers.
COLLECTION	1,400+ oral histories and growing actively (111 oral histories added in 2004). Digital video has replaced audiocassettes. Most oral histories conducted within program, but do more collaborative projects recently.
PHYSICAL SPACE	Share space with Carnegie Library for Local History.
INTERVIEWS	Conducted by volunteers trained and supported by the Program. Program Manager conducts regular individual and group meetings.
TRANSCRIPTS	Transcripts or summaries for most oral histories done by volunteers. Transcripts for some special projects funded by grants.
CATALOG	Program Manager and volunteers supply verified data for BPL cataloger to create MARC record for library OPAC.
PRESERVATION	All audio converted to .wav or MP3 files and stored on BPL servers. Preservation copies made and stored separately from user copies.
ACCESS	Reading room has a viewing station for local users. Highly developed website with audio and text, links to photographs, and the ability to search within an interview.
SECRETS TO SUCCESS	• Affiliated with supportive public library. • Enthusiastic and dedicated group of volunteers. • Monthly meetings allow volunteers to share work and learn from each other. • Comprehensive volunteer training program. • Innovative web presence through website and Google. • Paid manager to oversee program.
CHALLENGES	• Processing time slowed by duties to maintain digital archive and website. • Keeping up with technological changes. • Maintaining digital video equipment.

THE ORAL HISTORY PROJECT

The Vietnam Archive, Texas Tech University
Lubbock, Texas
http://www.vietnam.ttu.edu/oralhistory

MISSION/GOALS   To create and preserve a more complete record of the wars in Southeast Asia by preserving, through recorded interviews, the recollections and experiences of the participants, as well as those military and civilian personnel involved in activities surrounding the wars on the home front.

AGE   Since 1999, but donated interviews date back to the 1960s.

INSTITUTION   Oral History Project within university-based Vietnam Center and Archive.

FUNDING   Operational funds from the State of Texas.

STAFF   Two full-time oral historians have PhD in subject area. Additional paid staff, shared with Vietnam Archive, include transcribers, cataloger, and technical experts.

COLLECTION   530 interviews and growing. Most interviews conducted by staff oral historians in audio and transcribed; some video. Some donated interviews. Emphasis on preserving oral histories for the long term.

PHYSICAL SPACE   Share building space with the Southwest Collection/Special Collections Library. Includes space for staff offices, processing, and storage, as well as public reading/listening room.

INTERVIEWS   Conducted by subject specialists who are paid, full-time staff members. Majority of interviews are by telephone with narrators around the country, though some are conducted in person.

TRANSCRIPTS   Transcribed by staff, reviewed by interviewer and narrator.

CATALOG   Full MARC records created for TTU's online catalog and OCLC WorldCat.

PRESERVATION   A priority for this project. Emphasize transcripts, digital audio, prepare for format refreshment. Preservation copies maintained on-site in cold storage.

ACCESS   Since the project has a global audience in a remote physical location, digital archive emphasized. Goal is to post all materials on Vietnam Archive.

SECRETS TO SUCCESS
- Conduct full career interview, not just about activity in Southeast Asia.
- Remove restricted format limitations, thus allowing the freedom to conduct each interview on a person-by-person basis.
- Meticulous about having legal papers signed.
- In addition, obtain a recorded verbal Legal Disclosure and Interview Agreement for each interview.
- Supporting documents in Vietnam Archive to provide context for interview.

CHALLENGES
- Coordinating a program with over 2,100 participants.
- Meeting objective of quick turnaround time from "interview to archive."

UAF ORAL HISTORY PROGRAM

Elmer E. Rasmuson Library, University of Alaska
Fairbanks, Alaska
http://www.uaf.edu/library/oralhistory

MISSION/GOALS	To collect, preserve, and make available to the public recorded interviews of Alaskan interest.
AGE	Since 1981, but mission and goals changed along the way. Different stages in institutional life emphasized collecting, preservation, and access.
INSTITUTION	Oral history program within university library. Project Jukebox operates under the direction of oral history program, but with its own staff.
FUNDING	Combination of library budgets and grants.
STAFF	Curator/director (1.0 FTE) has PhD in subject area. Assistant curator (1.0 FTE) has MLS. Both are permanent employees. Assistant (.5 FTE) funded by library and grants. Three Project Jukebox staff (2.0 FTE total) funded by grants. Other functions shared with library staff.
COLLECTION	About 10,000 oral histories from 1940s on. About one-third on open-reel tape, two-thirds on audiocassette; one percent on video; newer ones born digital. Condition and archival control varies. Process about 200 oral histories each year. Most interviews (including current) on audiocassette.
PHYSICAL SPACE	Staff offices in a section of the library, along with circulating copies of interviews. Originals and preservation masters stored on another floor of the library.
INTERVIEWS	Interviews conducted by staff, donations from the community, or UAF student projects. UAF staff sometimes trains interviewers but there is not a formal training program.
TRANSCRIPTS	Transcription work and its quality varies. Transcription is desired but not a priority.
CATALOG	18 percent of the collection currently catalogued in MARC for local OPAC. Takes about three hours to create each catalog record; seven hours if interview summaries are made. Use has increased significantly due to cataloging.
PRESERVATION	Preservation priority comes after patron service and processing. Need outstrips the means, since more than 65 percent of the collection is from the 1980s or earlier, but staff are always mindful of preservation needs.
ACCESS	Project Jukebox online. Other oral histories described on library's OPAC.

SECRETS TO SUCCESS	Be true to two simple principles:
	    (1) patron comes first; and
	    (2) never lose a tape.

CHALLENGES	Maintaining older media formats currently in the collection. Anticipating and preparing for evolution in technology.

VETERANS' ORAL HISTORY PROJECT

Morse Institute Library
Natick, Massachusetts
http://www.natickvets.org/

MISSION/GOALS	To preserve the life stories of men and women veterans who live in and around Natick, Massachusetts.
AGE	Since 1998.
INSTITUTION	Oral history program within a public library.
FUNDING	Received start-up funding from the town of Natick. Ongoing operational costs dependent upon grants and donations. Have received support from veterans organizations in and around Natick.
STAFF	Community Relations Coordinator (1.0 FTE) manages project, in addition to other duties. VOH Project Coordinator (.5 FTE) conducts interviews and oversees their processing. This position is paid by grants and is dependent upon availability of funds.
COLLECTION	More than 150 visual histories and growing, as funds permit. Since operations depend on grants and donations, activity is uneven.
PHYSICAL SPACE	Morse Institute Library, Natick's public library, oversees this program. Space includes office for staff, room for filming interviews, climate-controlled vault for preservation copies of videos, and public reading/viewing room. User copies of videos are in circulating collection and used heavily.
INTERVIEWS	Community Relations Coordinator makes initial contact and describes oral history for potential narrators. Project Coordinator, trained in oral history, conducts video interviews. Sometimes a separate videographer operates the camera. Some oral histories are edited and enhanced; others stand as filmed.
TRANSCRIPTS	No funds for transcribing.
CATALOG	Full MARC records created for Natick's OPAC and local consortium, Minuteman Library Network.
PRESERVATION	We take preservation seriously. Preservation copy made in SVHS format, stored in library's climate-controlled vault. Prepared to migrate to new formats as they emerge.
ACCESS	Catalog records in library OPAC and Minuteman Library Network. Videotapes circulate and are checked out by local users and by interlibrary loan requests.
SECRETS TO SUCCESS	Making veterans comfortable; giving them the questions ahead of time to prepare (but not memorize). Whether the program continues or not, the quality of the interviews make it a successful oral history project.
CHALLENGES	Lack of consistent funding, thereby, the difficulty in retaining a part-time oral historian. Veterans are passing on without the opportunity to tell their stories.

APPENDIX B

FORMS

I selected or created these forms from hundreds of documents that I've reviewed in the past year. Use them as is or adapt them to the needs of your own project.

ACQUISITIONS GUIDELINES*

The Archives accepts donations of material for its research from individuals, organizations, and businesses.

When accepting material, the Archives is responsible for:

1. Maintaining the materials, ensuring accepted practice for preservation and security, preparing the materials for research use through professional arrangement and cataloging, and supplying them to any interested researcher on an equal basis during regular business hours.

2. Ensuring that all material containing confidential information is restricted from all use in accordance with the explicit instructions of the donor as long as the restriction is "reasonable" and affects all potential users equally. The Archives cannot accept collections that are restricted indefinitely, or for which the restriction cannot be enforced equally or with reasonable effort.

3. Making decisions about preserving and preparing collections consistent with professional archival practice to best serve the material itself, researchers, and this organization. Materials that the Archives wishes to remove from the collection will be discarded, offered to another institution, or returned to the donor according to the donor's instructions and institutional policies.

4. Securing legal documentation for every gift that makes clear the terms of the transfer and any instructions of the donor. The Archives will accept a deed of gift that transfers title to this organization. The Archives will honor all agreements with the donor.

The Archives cannot:

1. Accept donations without transfer of title.

2. Accept material for which the donor does not have clear title.

3. Provide appraisals of the monetary value of gifts. The Archives will provide the names of appraisers without recommendation to donors who wish to have materials appraised.

4. Accept liability for loss or damage of materials due to deterioration, fire, or other natural disasters.

*Reprinted with permission from the Society of American Archivists and ARMA International.

ACCESSION FORM FOR ORAL HISTORY COLLECTION*

Date Received	Accession No.	Other No.

Name of Collection

Source of Collection

Donor Contact Info (Name, Full address, Phone, Email)

Physical Location in Archive	Restrictions	

Content Description	Condition Description	Size Description

QUICK INVENTORY	QTY	SIZE	CONDITION
Recording Media			
Legal Consent Forms			
Transcripts			
Photos			
Other material (describe)			

Accompanying Documentation

Received by	Accession Date	Donor Form Received

Comments

*Adapted with permission from the Society of American Archivists and ARMA International.

SAMPLE COLLECTION POLICY*

UAF ORAL HISTORY PROGRAM
COLLECTION DEVELOPMENT POLICY

We define "oral history" as being the verbal recollection of an individual's life and/or the history of a particular region, community, industry, institution, or event.

Criteria for the acceptance of audiovisual (AV) materials into the collection include the following:

1.) Materials should be Alaska and/or Northern Regions related.

2.) Materials should have substantial content and/or provide unique insights into particular events or time periods.

3.) Materials should be of the highest possible listening/viewing quality. Materials so poorly recorded or degraded as to be difficult and/or impossible for the user to access will not be accepted.

4.) Materials should be accessible to users. Any restrictions put on the materials should not place undue burden upon the users and/or the library staff.

5.) Materials should be in a standard AV format that will be supported by the media industry for the foreseeable future. If materials are recorded on obsolete formats, they should be able to be converted to standard formats on equipment readily available at UAF. Because of technological obsolescence, we are unable to accept the following formats:

_____

_____

6.) Video recordings will be evaluated by the Film and Moving Images Curator and, if necessary, cross-referenced to both the Film Archives and the Oral History collections.

7.) Ideally, the following items should accompany tapes given to the UAF Oral History Program:

    1.) Transcript or summary of interview

    2.) UAF release form and/or letter of transmittal

    3.) Description of tape including narrator, interviewer, date, and location of interview. This information should be written on each tape label.

8.) The UAF Oral History Program reserves the right to reject any materials that are deemed unsuitable for its collection.

*Reproduced with permission from the University of Alaska, Fairbanks, Oral History Program

COLLECTION EVALUATION FOR ACCESSION

Collection Name or Description _____

Content Intellectual connection among the materials and to the existing collection.	
Legal papers Legal consent form signed and dated? Restrictions? Missing papers?	
Inventory List each physical medium and count (or estimate) the number within each category.	
Physical condition Make a visual assessment of the physical condition, for each section.	
Existing documentation Are media labeled? Is there an interview summary? Is current contact information available?	

Completed by _____   Date _____

PROCESSING CHECKLIST

Narrator	Interviewer
Name	**Name**
Contact Info	**Contact Info**
Interview Date	

Date Rcd		Notes
	Original recording	
	Legal Consent Form	
	Recording Copied	
	Media labeled	
	Sent for Transcription	
	Transcript Rcd	
	Audit-check Transcript	
	Transcript to Narrator	
	Transcript Approved	
	Print transcript/Assemble supplementary Materials/Bind	
	Digitize recording	
	Catalog record	
	Deposit into Archive	

BASIC CONSENT FORM

WE, <u>narrator,</u> and <u>interviewer,</u> give our consent to <u>the oral history program/archive</u> to use all or any part of our interview and supplementary materials in any format for scholarly, educational, or community awareness purposes. We give all literary rights, including copyright, <u>to oral history program/archive</u>. However, this does not apply to our own use: we may use recorded interviews or the information contained in them as we wish.

We further understand that copies of the recording and transcript will be deposited in the <u>archive</u> to be available for public listening, reading and viewing, and that portions of our interview may be used in publications, documentaries, and on the Internet.

We release <u>archive/oral history program</u> from all claims arising out of, or in connection with the use of our observations, memories, and experiences. We understand that the <u>archive/oral history program</u> cannot be held liable for the use of information by third parties who may extract portions of our words for their own creative work.

The purpose of the interview is to document the narrator's experiences <u>topic of interview</u>. The interview will not exceed <u>maximum length</u> min. in length. Our participation is entirely voluntary.

Interview date _____

PLEASE PRINT

Narrator	Interviewer
Name _____	_____
Address _____	_____
_____	_____
Phone/email _____	_____
Signed _____	_____
Date _____	_____

SAMPLE CONSENT FORM*

D E N S H Ō
The Japanese American Legacy Project

Interview Release Form

Thank you for agreeing to be interviewed by Denshō, a Washington not-for-profit corporation.

The goal of Denshō is to document the Japanese American experience for research, education, and historic preservation. Potential uses of the interviews (in whole or in part) include, but are not limited to, incorporation in the following: an archive to be made available worldwide via digital networks, educational curriculum, film or video documentaries, online computer websites, publications, disc-based products, promotional or fundraising materials, and museum exhibits. In addition, interviews may be made available to other entities with similar educational or historical purposes.

By signing this form, you are hereby relinquishing and assigning to Denshō all legal title and literary property rights in the Denshō interview(s) in which you participated (including: video and audio tapes, transcripts, interview notes, and any images or information contained therein). Rights assigned to Denshō through this agreement include copyright, and more particularly, the exclusive rights to publish, exhibit, display, assign, license, transfer with or without consideration, reproduce, edit, distribute, and use in derivative works. Denshō may exercise such rights itself or through third parties it shall select in its sole discretion.

You also are agreeing to release Denshō, its officers, directors, employees, agents and associations, from any and all liability for damages for libel, slander, invasion of privacy, and any other claims based on the publication, exhibition, display, copyright, license, transfer, reproduction, editing, disposition, or other use of your interview(s).

It is also your understanding that you will not receive compensation for the use of your name and interview(s), but your consideration is that this valuable material will benefit the Japanese American community and people worldwide now and in the future. In appreciation, Denshō staff will mail you a VHS videotape copy of your interview(s) for your personal viewing. Thank you again for participating with Denshō.

Interview Date(s):_____

Read and agreed to this _____ **day of** _____, 20_____

(Signature)_____

*Reproduced with permission from Denshō: The Japanese American Legacy Project.

SAMPLE INTERVIEWER GIFT TO ARCHIVE*

Donated Oral History Collection
Regional Oral History Office

The Bancroft Library
University of California
Berkeley, California 94720

INTERVIEWER'S GIFT TO THE BANCROFT LIBRARY

    I, _____ (Interviewer), do hereby give to the Regents of the University of California for such scholarly and educational purposes as the Director of The Bancroft Library may determine, copies of the tapes and transcripts of the interviews listed on the attached Exhibit, including the right to publish all or any portion of such material and to authorize others to publish quotations.

    This gift does not preclude any use which I or the narrator of each interview may want to make of the recordings of his or her interview(s).

    Dated: _____

_____

Interviewer

_____

_____

_____

Name & Address of Interviewer

Accepted for the Bancroft Library by:

_____

Division Head
Regional Oral History Office

_____

Dated

_____

Subject of Interview(s)

*Reproduced with permission from the Regional Oral History Office, Bancroft Library, University of California.

SAMPLE DEED OF GIFT TO THE PUBLIC DOMAIN*

UNITED STATES SENATE ORAL HISTORY PROJECT

Deed of Gift:

I, _narrator's name_, do hereby give to the Senate Historical Office the tape recordings and transcripts of my interviews _interview dates_. I authorize the Senate Historical Office to use the tapes and transcripts in such a manner as may best serve the educational and historical objectives of their oral history program. I also approve the deposits of the transcripts at the Library of Congress, National Archives, Senate Library and any other institution which the Senate Historical Office may deem appropriate. Selected portions of the transcripts will remain closed until _date_. I voluntarily convey ownership of the tapes and transcripts to the public domain.

Narrator's name _____

Date _____

Accepted on behalf of the Senate Historical Office by: _____

*Reproduced with permission, U.S. Senate Oral History Project

SAMPLE CONSENT TO PUBLISH*

CENTER FOR SOUTHWEST RESEARCH
UNIVERSITY LIBRARIES, THE UNIVERSITY OF NEW MEXICO
PERMISSION TO PUBLISH OR USE REPRODUCTIONS OF MATERIALS

NAME _____

ADDRESS _____

CITY _____ STATE _____ ZIP CODE _____

PHONE NO. _____ FAX _____ EMAIL _____

I/We request permission to publish, exhibit, or broadcast the following item(s) from the collections of the Center for Southwest Research, The University of New Mexico:

Collection # _____ Collection Name _____

Description of items _____

Title or description of publication/name/place of exhibit _____

Format (book, magazine, TV/film, web) _____

Where possible, CSWR requests either a copy of the published work or notification of the date and location of the broadcast, or the name and date of the media wherein published.

I/We_____ agree that

- Permission is for one time use only, including electronic use, for the express purpose described above and that further use will require separate written permission from the Center for Southwest Research.

- The Center for Southwest Research does not control the rights or reproduction for all materials in its collection. I/We assume all responsibility for obtaining reproduction rights, including obtaining permissions to use material protected by copyright.

- I/We will credit the Center for Southwest Research, The University of New Mexico as follows: [Document, plan, photo, etc.], [Name of Collection], Center for Southwest Research, University Libraries, The University of New Mexico.

My/Our signature(s) indicates that I/we have read and accepted the conditions set forth above.

Signature _____ Date _____

Signature of ARR Reference person _____Date _____

*Reprinted with permission form the Center for Southwest Research, University Libraries, University of New Mexico.

SAMPLE CONSENT TO PUBLISH ON THE INTERNET*

THE **MARIA ROGERS**

Oral History Program

OF THE CARNEGIE BRANCH LIBRARY FOR LOCAL HISTORY

GREETINGS! We are writing to you because, some years ago, you completed an oral history for the Maria Rogers Oral History Program (or a related program) that is archived at the Carnegie Branch Library for Local History of the Boulder Public Library.

There has been an exciting technological development at the Boulder Public Library. By the end of this year (2003) we expect to be able to make the audio portion of all our interviews accessible via the internet, along with the text of interview summaries and transcripts. This means that you, your friends and family members, researchers, and other interested individuals will be able to listen to the oral history interviews without having to come to the Carnegie Library.

Because the internet was not as developed as a conduit for information—or perhaps did not even exist—when you did your interview, **we are writing now to give you the opportunity to opt in or out of having your interview posted on the library's web site.**

Please let us know your wishes by filling out the form below and returning it to:
Maria Rogers Oral History Program / Carnegie Branch Library
1125 Pine St. / Boulder, CO 80302-4024

If we do not hear from you by _____, we will assume that we have permission for including your interview on our web site. You can, of course, change your permission status at any time. If you have any questions, please feel free to contact me at 303-441-3110 (phone), 303-441-1981 (voice-mail), or beckers@boulder.lib.co.us (email).

Susan Becker, Oral History Program Manager

---

1. Please CHECK ONE:

____ I, _____, hereby give permission for the Boulder Public Library to make my oral history interview(s), (Call Number(s): _____), accessible via the internet.

OR

____ I do NOT give permission for the above-named interview(s) to be made accessible via the internet.

2. IF you DO give permission for internet access, check item below, if you wish:

____ I would like to have my interview linked to a photo of me and have enclosed a photo that you may scan for the web site and place in my file.

3. Please sign: PRINT Name _____ Date _____

Signature _____ Phone Number _____

*Reproduced with permission from the Maria Rogers Oral History Program.

SAMPLE ONLINE SITE USE AGREEMENT*

Gates of the Arctic Jukebox Program
Use of Project Jukebox Programs

The University of Alaska Fairbanks Oral History Program holds copyright to the recordings and transcripts. The Oral History program has special permission to use the images included in this program and we thank all of our contributors for their help. We provide access to these materials strictly for educational and research purposes. The fact that recordings, images and transcripts are posted on this site provides public access to them, but does not constitute a right to copy, make a profit from or publish these oral history materials. No use (beyond limited quotation) should be made of these interviews without the express permission of the UAF Oral History Program. Permission must be obtained for publication of any material beyond that which might jeopardize the integrity or value of the whole copyrighted work, as covered in the Fair Use portion of United States Copyright Law. To gain permission write Oral History Curator at UAF Oral History Program, Elmer E. Rasmuson Library, UAF, P.O. Box 756808 Fairbanks, AK 99775 or call 907-474-5355.

We ask that researchers approach the material with respect for, and awareness of the cultures and individuals whose lives, ideas, and creativity are represented here. Because of the dangers of cross-cultural misunderstandings, we encourage users to become knowledgeable in the cultural backgrounds of the speakers before interpreting and referencing these works in print or media publications. Users are strongly encouraged to consult the *Guidelines for Respecting Cultural Knowledge* established by the Assembly of Alaska Native Educators and the Principles and Standards of the Oral History Association.

Site Use Agreement

As a user of this site, you agree to:
1) Not use the material for commercial purposes. Short quotes and references are permitted for instructional and publication purposes.

2) Provide complete citations referencing speaker, interviewer, date, tape number, jukebox program, and Website with URL Address.

3) Not re-post or link this site or any parts of it to another program or listing, without permission.

4) Follow the *Guidelines for Respecting Cultural Knowledge* and the *Principles and Standards of the Oral History Association.*

Unauthorized attempts to upload information or change information on this site are strictly prohibited and may be punishable under the Computer Fraud and Abuse Act of 1986 and the National Information Infrastructure Protection Act of 1995.

AGREE	DO NOT AGREE

* Reproduced with permission from the University of Alaska Fairbanks, Oral History Program. Online version at http://uaf-db.uaf.edu/Jukebox/PJWeb/progusecc.htm.

*Reproduced with permission from the University of Alaska Fairbanks, Oral History Program. Online version at http://uaf-db.uaf.edu/Jukebox/PJWeb/progusecc.htm.

TRANSCRIBING PLAN

1. Collection: What needs to be transcribed?

2. Preparation. Are recordings in a format that can be sent to transcribers (currently audiocassette or digital sound file)?

3. Extent. How many recorded hours? How many physical items?

4. Workflow/Timeframe: Map out all the steps for the transcription process, with a turnaround or completion time for each.

5. Resources: Are there funds for transcription? Can staff members or volunteers transcribe? Is transcription equipment/software available?

6. What additional tasks should transcribers do?
   - ❑ Audit-check
   - ❑ Research spelling of proper names
   - ❑ Chapter/section headings
   - ❑ Table of contents
   - ❑ Index
   - ❑ Other

7. What additional materials will be included in the transcript? Who will do this work?
   - ❑ Photos
   - ❑ Biographical material
   - ❑ Historical material
   - ❑ Other

8. Are there known difficulties with any recordings
   - ❑ Poor sound quality
   - ❑ Foreign language speakers
   - ❑ Interviews or sections of interviews missing
   - ❑ Background noise makes speakers hard to hear

Oral History Project or Institution _____

Completed by _____ Date _____

TRANSCRIBING PROTOCOL

ADMINISTRATIVE

Curator's contact information:

Transcriber or agency's contact information:

Funding:
- ❑ Transcriber's fees (per transcript, per page, or per hour)
- ❑ Source of funding

Equipment:
- ❑ Transcribing machine (for audiocassettes)
- ❑ Provided by transcriber   ❑ Provided by archive
- ❑ Transcribing software. Specify name and version _____

Office space/computer required for transcribing (if done in-house):

File structure, naming protocol for transcripts:

Deadlines (completion of project, end of funding, etc.):

WORKFLOW

Make copy of original recordings for transcriber

Delivery method:
- ❑ Recording to transcriber _____

- ❑ Transcript to archive _____

Expected turnaround time _____

TRANSCRIBER'S RESPONSIBILITIES & INSTRUCTIONS

❑ Computer software and version

❑ Instructions for electronic delivery of transcript

❑ Style Guide

❑ Added tasks
   Audit-check
   Chapter headings
   Table of contents
   Index
   Verify content. Specify _____
   Other

❑ Instructions for returning recording and transcript

Oral History Project or Institution _____

Completed by _____ Date _____

SAMPLE TRANSCRIBERS' GUIDE*

Our interview transcripts provide an accurate rendering of the *intellectual* content of the interview, and serve as the ultimate preservation format. Transcripts are not a substitute for the audio interview, the primary document and the most complete capture of the narrator's experience, but rather a tool to quickly find relevant sections of the recording, and a back-up to verify hard-to-hear sections and the spelling of names. With this in mind, please transcribe every meaningful word, but not necessarily "umms," false starts, repetitions and other extraneous sounds.

REMINDER: All interview content is confidential until approved by the narrator.

GENERAL

The program coordinator will "e-introduce" you to the interviewer via email. You two should communicate directly for questions about the recording. Clarifying things as you go can save a lot of time in the future.

The program manager will send you a packet with a) the audiocassette recording, b) the Contact Data Form with names correctly spelled and interview dates, c) list of proper names and foreign words, if provided by the interviewer, and c) a blank invoice form for you to complete.

Transcribing machines are available for check-out from the library.

SETTING UP THE DOCUMENT

- **WORD PROCESSING PROGRAM:** MS Word 98 or higher

- **FONT:** Times New Roman

- **SIZE:** 11 pt. for text, 14 pt. for title

- **SPACING:** 1.5 spacing throughout text. Add one extra space between speakers.

- **INTERVIEWER'S VOICE:** Put interviewer's voice in *italics.*

- **MARGINS:** Use default margins *except:* change footer margin to .65".

- **INDENT:** In the Format -> Paragraph section, set Special to "Hanging Indent"

- **HEADER AND FOOTER:**
  Header should include the full name of the narrator in upper case at the left, and the words "TRANSCRIPT, INTERVIEW [date of interview]" at the right.

  Footer should have the words "transcribed by [your name] at the left, the page number in the middle and the date of transcription at the right.

- DOCUMENT PROPERTIES: File -> Properties -> Summary
  Title: [name of interviewee] interview, [unless provided by archivist]
  Subject: [Name of interviewee]
  Author: [Name of interviewer]
  Manager: [Name of transcriber]
  Company: Oakland Living History Program
  Category: Project [e.g., Grace Shibata Oral History Project]
  Comments: [date of interview]
          [# in series, e.g., "interview 2 of 3"]
          [date transcription is complete]

- TITLE: Title should be 14 pt., aligned center. Should read:

OAKLAND LIVING HISTORY PROGRAM
INTERVIEW TRANSCRIPT

- AT HEAD OF TRANSCRIPT: Begin the transcript with the initials and the names of the interviewee and interviewer, and anyone else on the recording, as follows:

  MN: Marion Newhall, interviewer
  SB: Stephanie Martinez, narrator
  For the remainder, use initials in upper case, followed by a colon.

- INAUDIBLE WORDS OR PROBLEMS FOR INTERVIEWER TO REVIEW: Type inaudible passages, foreign words, words with questionable spellings in red, to alert the interviewer. Indicate inaudible in red by passages by "[inaudible]"

STYLE GUIDE

- Transcribe every meaningful word, but use your judgment regarding pauses, repetitions, and false starts. You are recording the intellectual content of the interview, not reproducing the interview itself.

- Indicate interruptions to the interview if they are relevant by a bracketed phrase: e.g., [telephone rings and Mr. ___ answers it, interview resumes], [Mr. ___'s spouse enters the room and joins the interview]

- Keep paragraphs short. Begin a new paragraph for every new thought.

- Use judgment with punctuation; attempt to capture the narrator's intent, but also keep the transcript readable. Use full stop at the end of a thought, even if the speaker continues on.

- The style guide for this project is *The Chicago manual of style*, 15th ed. (Chicago: University of Chicago Press, 2003). Consult the *Manual* with regard to spelling, punctuation, capitalization, and numeration, and proper names. In particular, consult Sections 6-9 (grammar and usage, punctuation, spelling, distinctive treatment of words and compounds, names and terms, and numbers).

- Type foreign words in *italics*. Always verify spelling/transliteration with interviewer.

When you are finished

- Review transcript for spelling, punctuation, and format. (You do not need to listen to the tape with the transcript in hand; the interviewer will do that.) Make sure you have indicated problem areas in red type.

- Save the document electronically until the end of the project. The archivist will notify you to delete the file once the final copy is approved and in the archive.

- Send an electronic copy of the transcript to the interviewer and the archivist.

- Return the tape and the invoice to the archivist.

THANK YOU VERY MUCH!

CATALOGING PLAN

1. ACCESS TO LIBRARY. Is the oral history project connected to a library that agrees to catalog for them?

2. CATALOG HOME. Where will catalog records live? Consider all the possibilities for exposure to your catalog: in-house database, bibliographic utility, library OPAC, consortium, World Wide Web.

3. CATALOGERS. Who will do the cataloging and what are their relevant skills?

4. COLLECTION. What exactly needs to be catalogued and how should it be represented?

5. CONTENT. How detailed should catalog records be and what information should be included?

6. WORKFLOW/TIMEFRAME. Will oral histories be catalogued in a batch or over time? Is the oral history project complete or ongoing? Approximately how many oral histories should be catalogued per month/year?

7. COST. Who pays for cataloging?

8. INSTITUTIONAL REQUIREMENTS. Special requirements of parent institution or funding agency.

Oral History Project or Institution _____

Completed by _____ Date _____

CATALOGING PROTOCOL

ADMINISTRATIVE

Contact for oral history:

Contact for cataloging:

Source of funding:

Deadlines/Reports/Requirements of funder or administration:

Oral Historian's Responsibilities

1. Quantity: how many oral histories per month/year? Deliver as a batch or as received?
2. Delivery method (recordings/transcripts/worksheets):
3. Required information:
4. Instructions for call number/physical address:

CATALOG

1. Where do catalog records live?
2. Expected turnaround time or deadline for completion:
3. Encoding format and standards:
4. Bibliographic unit (interview/oral history/collection):
5. Relationship to other institutions or catalogs:
6. Who catalogs:
7. Instructions for indexing:
8. Instructions for controlled vocabulary terms:
9. Constant data in bibliographic record:
10. Special instructions:

BIBLIOGRAPHIC RECORD

1. Who is considered primary author (main entry)?
2. Title:
3. Oral history project:
4. Parent institution:
5. Physical description:
6. Summary:
7. Subject terms:
8. Added entries:

Oral History Project or Institution _____

Completed by _____ Date _____

CATALOGING WORKSHEET #1

Be sure names, spellings, and dates are accurate. Incorrect or incomplete information at this point will be perpetuated through the catalog record and any subsequent use of the oral history materials.

Narrator's name (100)*+:

Interviewer's name (700)+:

Title of oral history (245)*:

Interview date(s) (260, 518):

Interview location(s) (518):

Item catalogued (300)*:

Accompanying items (300)*:

Summary of interview content (520):

Narrator biographical summary (545):

Subject keywords (6xx)+:

Name of oral history program (710)+#:

Sponsoring institution (710)+#:

Access/restrictions notes (540)#:

Series/Relationships (4xx, 8xx)+#:

Physical/Online locations (530, 856):

\# Constant data

* Required fields defined locally in Cataloging Protocol

\+ Indexed terms defined locally in Cataloging Protocol

CATALOGING WORKSHEET #2

Accession Number: OH_____

Narrator: _____ Date of birth: _____

Interviewer: _____ Filmed by: _____

INTERVIEW SUMMARY.

BIOGRAPHICAL SUMMARY.

PLACE NAMES.

PERSONAL NAMES.

TOPICS.

Catalog record prepared by: _____

Date completed: _____

SAMPLE MARC RECORD*

LEADER 00000nim 2200000Ia 4500
001   ocm52760733
003   OCoLC
005   20030731105157.0
007   ss lmnjlc---na
008   030731s2003   cau n   t eng d
040   MIQ|cMIQ
043   n-us-ca
049   MIQA
092   378.794 |b MOpc
100 1 Catlett, Frances Dunham, |d 1908- |4 ive
245 10 Frances Dunham Catlett interview |h [sound recording] : |b an oral history.
260 |c 2003.
300   1 audiocassette :|b analog
300   1 transcript (30 p.) ; |c 28 cm.
440 0 Mills College class projects ; |v 2003
440 0 African American history of Mills alumna
500   These interviews comprise part of a senior thesis project by Angelle Pryor.
500   Interview conducted on April 17, 2003 by Angelle Pryor.
520   Ms. Catlett discusses her experiences at Mills College as an African American student in the 1940s.
535 1 Special Collections, F.W. Olin Library, Mills College; |b 5000 MacArthur Blvd., Oakland, CA94613
535 2 Oakland History Room, Oakland Public Library; |b 125 14th Street, Oakland, CA94612
536   Funded as part of a three year project by the James Irvine Foundation
540   Written permission to use materials in whole or part, in any format must be obtained in writing from the Oakland Living History Program at Mills College.
545 0 Frances Dunham Catlett, class of '47 is the first African American graduate of Mills College. She is a visual artist living in the San Francisco Bay Area.
520   This interview focuses on Ms. Catlett's experience at Mills College in the 1940s, especially as an African American woman in a traditionally white college
600 10 Catlett, Frances Dunham,|d1908- |v Interviews.
610 20 Mills College |x Alumnae and alumni |v Interviews.
610 20 Mills College |x History.
650 0 African American college students |v Interviews.
650 0 Women college students |v Interviews.
655 0 Oral history.
700 1 Pryor, Angelle.|4 ivr
710 2 Oakland Living History Program.

LOCATION	CALL #	STATUS
College Archive	378.794 MOpc transcript	CHECKED IN
College Archive	378.794 MOpc CD	CHECKED IN

* Reproduced with permission from the Oakland Living History Program, Mills College

COLLECTION EVALUATION FOR PRESERVATION*

Institution or Collection _____

PHYSICAL MEDIUM				
Other analog formats				
Other digital formats				
Transcripts				

STORAGE AREA

❑ Separate stack area ❑ Departmental office ❑ Closets/File Cabinets ❑ Another part of the building

❑ Offsite climate controlled storage ❑ Offsite, not climate controlled

❑ Digital storage only

STORAGE AREA CONDITIONS

❑ Climate controlled: Temperature maintained at _____degrees; humidity maintained at _____ %

❑ Adequate ventilation and air filter ❑ Smoke detector ❑ Sprinkler system ❑ Protection from insect or rodent infestation ❑ Light controlled

---

SECURITY

❑ Storage room locked? ❑ Alarmed? Who has access _____

❑ Storage separate from reading room? ❑ Researchers monitored at all times?

❑ Written disaster plan? Last updated _____

❑ For archive only ❑ For parent institution

Completed by _____ Date _____

*Adaped by permission of the Society of American Archivists and ARMA International.

ITEM-LEVEL EVALUATION FOR PRESERVATION*

Accession #		

This is ☐ Only copy ☐ Original ☐ Preservation master ☐ User copy ☐ Other
Location

☐ Additional interviews on other media. How many _____ Location _____
Comments:

Medium ☐ Open reel ☐ Audiocassette ☐ DAT ☐ Minidisc ☐ CD ☐ DVD
☐ Other

☐ Duplicate copies. What medium _____ Location _____
Comments:

Transcript? ☐ Yes ☐ No
Comments:

Digitized ? ☐ Yes ☐ No Date _____
Comments:

Physical condition: ☐ Excellent ☐ Good ☐ Fair ☐ Poor
☐ Spliced ☐ Sticky ☐ Flaking ☐ Needs repair
Comments:

Sound quality: ☐ Excellent ☐ Good ☐ Fair ☐ Poor
Comments:

Recommendations:
☐ Repair media ☐ Restore sound ☐ Direct transfer ☐ Do not play
Comments:

Action #1 Date/Initials

Action #2 Date/Initials

Completed by _____ Date _____

*Adapted by permission of the Society of American Archivists and ARMA International.

PRESERVATION PLANNING CHECKLIST

PROCESS	
GOALS ❏ Rescue deteriorating media ❏ Participate in collaborative digitization project ❏ Digitize for Internet access and preservation ❏ New collection needs special preservation attention ❏ Institutional mandate ❏ Preservation part of general collection management	
WORKFLOW ISSUES ❏ Outsource ❏ Complete work onsite ❏ One-time effort ❏ Ongoing ❏ Collaborative project ❏ Our collection only ❏ Restoration work required ❏ Format transfer only ❏ Metadata standards ❏ Digital transfer specifications ❏ Project management system for tracking work Deadline for completion _____	
OUTCOME ❏ Move original recordings to offsite storage ❏ User copies located _____ ❏ Formats of copies _____ ❏ Internet access to collection	
RESOURCES, HUMAN If outsourced: ❏ Administrative liaison ❏ Content liaison If onsite: ❏ Project manager ❏Technical manager ❏ Technicians	
RESOURCES, TECHNICAL ❏ Format transfer equipment ❏ Recording media ❏ Computer hardware ❏ Computer software ❏ Mass storage servers	

RESOURCES, FINANCIAL
Grant funds: ❏ Ongoing ❏ One-time (how long) _____
    Requirements: _____
Institutional funds: ❏ Ongoing ❏ Limited time _____
    Requirements: _____	

MAINTENANCE ❏ What needs to be done and when ❏ Project management system for tracking ❏ Allocate funds for maintenance ❏ Who will do the maintenance	

Completed by _____   Date _____

APPENDIX C
GLOSSARY–TERMS AND ACRONYMS

Acronyms are so common today that the original terms often get lost or changed, and no one can remember the original meaning. This glossary contains terms and acronyms from the various technical vocabularies from fields that curators must draw upon in their work with oral histories. They are listed the way they are most commonly used—for example, CD, not compact disc, but Cultural Resource Management, not CRM; but there are always cross-references from one to the other. Any term in **bold** has its own entry. The specific area within oral history to which the term applies is also noted.

This glossary is also available online, with hotlinks to connect the cross references, at http://www.nancymackay.net/curating/glossary.htm.

AACR. *See* **Anglo American Cataloging Rules**.

access. (Archives) The ability to locate information through finding aids, catalogs, or websites. Access is one of the five principles of good archival practice.

access point. (Cataloging) A name, term, phrase, or code used as a heading in a catalog, such as author or subject. *See also* **index term**.

accessibility. (Archives) The availability of archival materials for consultation. Accessibility is determined by legal authorization, proximity of materials to researchers, usable formats, or the existence of finding aids.

accession. (Archives) The act of formally and legally accepting a single oral history, or oral history collection, into an archive.

accession number. (Archives) A unique number assigned to a document in an archive, to connect it from the catalog record or finding aid to the physical item on the shelf. *See also* **address**, **call number**.

acid-free paper. (Preservation) Paper with a pH of 7.0 or greater at the time of manufacture. Acid-free paper is the standard for long-term preservation, and most paper manufactured today is acid-free.

acid migration. (Preservation) The movement of acid from an item to something of lesser acidity, either from direct contact or through exposure to acidic vapors in the surrounding environment.

address. (Cataloging) The number or designation that connects the item described in the catalog to the physical item on the shelf. It can be an **accession number** (archives term), **call number** (library term), or **URL** (Information technology).

AMC format (MARC Format for Archival and Manuscripts Control). (Cataloging) A subset of **MARC format** endorsed by the Society of American Archivists for describing archival (unpublished) materials in a *library catalog*. **EAD** is the metadata scheme used for describing archival materials on the **World Wide Web**.

analog. (Recording technology) A process that records and stores sound in a continuous pattern, as it occurs in nature. Analog recording is being phased out in favor of **digital**, both for capture and for preservation, though the majority of oral histories in archives today are analog.

Anglo-American Cataloguing Rules (AACR). (Cataloging) Set of rules long accepted by the library world for cataloging materials generally found in libraries. AACR may be phased out in favor or other standards more appropriate to 21st century information needs. Rules for sound recordings and archival materials can be adapted for cataloging oral histories. *See also* **FRBR (Functional Requirements for Bibliographic Records)** and **RDA (Resource Description and Access)**.

archival quality. (Preservation) Physical qualities of materials, such as paper and recording media, that contribute to its long-term preservation under environmentally favorable conditions. This term is being phased out in favor of the term **life expectancy**, which is based on quantifiable measures.

archives. (Archives) 1. The actual materials to be saved. 2. The building or repository where archival materials are located. 3. The agency responsible for selecting, acquiring, preserving, and making available archival materials.

archivist. (Archives) The person responsible for the everyday functioning of an archive, including accessioning new collections, creating finding aids and other access tools, and managing use of archival materials. In smaller institutions, most archivists also take on curatorial duties. *See also* **curator**.

arrangement. (Archives) The process of organizing materials with respect to their **provenance** and **original order**, to protect their context and to achieve physical or intellectual control.

audiocassette. (Recording technology) An inexpensive and convenient container for audiotape. Audiocassettes were widely used for recording oral histories from the 1960s through the 1990s and most oral histories in archives today are stored on audiocassettes.

audit-check. (Oral history) Process of reviewing a transcript while listening to the recording, to catch transcription errors.

authentication protocol. (Information technology) Procedures that networked computers use to make sure only approved users have access to the Internet site. The most common authentication method is through user IDs and passwords.

authority control. (Cataloging) The process of establishing a unique and agreed-upon form for access points in a catalog record, such as personal, corporate, and geographic names, and subjects. A standard term for access points makes information retrieval in a database more precise. *See also* **controlled vocabulary**, **thesaurus**.

backlog. (Archives) An accumulation of tasks that need to be done to make archival materials available to the public.

bibliographic control. (Archives) A term almost synonymous with cataloging, a method for keeping track of the bibliographic elements of an item: the narrator, interviewer, number of physical items and the **address**. *See also* **intellectual control**.

bibliographic description. (Cataloging) The part of the catalog record that *describes* the physical and intellectual content of the item: the narrator, the interviewer, the dates of interview, and the physical items included. Other parts of the record can include **access points**, administrative data, and computer metadata.

bibliographic unit. (Cataloging) The item described in a catalog record, as defined by the cataloger or the oral historian. Usually a single oral history—a series of interviews of a single person—constitutes the bibliographic unit, but it could be a single interview (more precise) or a whole collection of interviews (more general).

bibliographic utility. (Cataloging) A network consisting of a large database of catalog records from diverse institutions, available online. **OCLC** is the largest bibliographic utility, known to public users as WorldCat and available in most libraries.

biographical data sheet. (Oral history) A form with specific information about the narrator, such as birth date and place, names of family members, and dates of major life events. This information helps the interviewer structure the interview and helps the cataloger record pertinent facts for the catalog record.

Boolean logic. (Information technology) A term used in Information Retrieval Systems that includes the logical operators "and," "or," "not," etc., which may be combined in a variety of ways to achieve precision in searching. Online databases usually call Boolean searching the "advanced search" screen.

born digital. (Preservation) A document created in a digital form, such as a text document created in a word processor, or an interview recorded on digital media.

broadcast quality. (Recording technology) Specifications defined by the National Television Standards Committee and the Advanced Television Systems Committee of the Federal Communications Commission for the level of quality at which radio or television stations will transmit.

browser. (Information technology) Computer program that allows users to locate, display, and link to and from **websites** on the **World Wide Web**. The most popular browsers are Internet Explorer and Firefox.

call number. (Cataloging) A number assigned to an item to connect it from the catalog to the physical item in the archive. It can be based on a standard classification system such as Dewey Decimal or Library of Congress, or on a local system. *See also* **address, accession number**.

cardioid microphone. *See* **directional/omnidirectional microphone**.

catalog. (Cataloging) A "container," usually a database, for catalog records that are related in some way, such as in a library, a digital archive, or a subject database. Records in the catalog can be searched and retrieved. The most common catalogs are library **OPAC**s, which consist of all the items in a particular library.

CD (Compact disc). (Recording technology) An optical medium for recording and storing data. Discs can have different qualities that are confusing to most of us (see table below). CDs look like DVDs but behave differently. *See also* **DVD**.

clip-on/desktop microphone. (Recording technology) As the name suggests, a clip-on microphone (also called a *lavaliere*) is a unidirectional **microphone** that can be clipped to the clothing of the speaker. Though it has a better chance of capturing the speaker's voice, it has certain hazards: (1) the speaker may turn away from the microphone and the sound is lost; (2) the microphone may flop over and not be able to record the speaker's voice. A desktop microphone sits on the table between the speakers and captures all the sound in the room. Though it is less sensitive to the voices of the speakers, there is less room for error.

collection. (Archives) A group of documents that are related in some way, such as the papers of a person, or an oral history series. The collection should be processed as a single unit, with a description of the collection as a whole and relationships among individual components.

collection policy. (Archives) A written statement that clearly states the purpose and the boundaries of the archive's collection goals.

collection level record. (Cataloging) A catalog record that describes an entire collection instead of an individual item—a collection of oral histories in a single record. *See also* **item-level record**.

collection management system. *See* **management system**.

compact disc. *See* **CD**.

compressed/uncompressed data. (Recording technology) Digital data can be compressed to reduce the size of the file and is usually done for transporting data over the Internet.

Disc	Type	Storage	Used for
CD-ROM, AudioCD	Read only	650 MB	Commercial use: computer programs, music
CD-R	Record once	650-700 MB (72 minutes of sound)	Recording sound or data
CD-RW	Rewritable	650-700MB (72 minutes of sound)	Not recommended for oral history recording or preservation

There is some loss of quality in compression, so it should not be used for preservation.

condenser microphone. *See* **dynamic/condenser microphone**.

consent form. *See* **legal consent form**.

conservation. (Preservation) The component of preservation that deals with the physical or chemical treatment of documents. *See also* **preservation**.

content. (Information technology) The *intellectual* information in a document, catalog, or collection, as contrasted to the format or structure. The distinction between structure and content is an important one for cataloging and preservation decisions. *See also* **structure**.

content management system. *See* **management system**.

contract. (Law) A legally binding agreement involving two or more parties, requiring some kind of consideration (payment), and specifying what each party will or will not do. Transfer of oral histories is more likely exchanged through a deed of gift, which does not require payment. *See also* **deed of gift**.

controlled vocabulary. (Cataloging) A list of words and phrases, also known as a **thesaurus**, showing synonymous, hierarchical, and other relationships to an authorized term which is indexed. The Library of Congress Subject Heading list is an example. A controlled vocabulary makes it much easier to retrieve information in a catalog or database. *See also* **authority control**.

copyright. (Law) The exclusive right to reproduce, publish, or sell copies of original creations (such as oral history interviews), and to **license** their production and sale by others. Copyright is granted by the federal government for a limited period of time. Once the term of copyright has expired, a work is in the **public domain**. When oral histories are accepted into an archive, copyright is usually transferred to the archive through a **deed of gift**. *See also* **intellectual property**.

copying. (Preservation) An important preservation principle (also known as "Lots of copies keeps stuff safe") referring to reproducing the content of an interview. Copies can be made from one format to another, or from one medium to another, to achieve something exactly the same as the original. *See also* **refresh**, **migrate**.

CRM. *See* **cultural resource management**.

cross reference. (Cataloging) A term used in catalogs, thesauruses, and indexes to lead you from one form of entry to a preferred or related one, such as the *see also* reference at the end of this entry. Cross references are an important feature of a catalog and make information retrieval more precise. *See also* **syndetic structures**, **hyperlink.**

cutural heritage. (Oral history) The history, beliefs, stories, ceremonies, law, language, symbols, land, and artifacts that are shared by a group of people and that make up their culture.

cultural resource management (CRM). (Management) The discipline devoted to the identification, maintenance, documentation, and preservation of significant cultural sites.

curation. (Archives) The long-term management and care of historical documents, in order to ensure wide access into the future.

curator. (Archives) The person responsible for the overall care and preservation of a collection. Tasks include fundraising and budgeting, collection policy, cataloging policy, short- and long-term preservation planning, compliance with professional and institutional standards, rights management, evaluating permission requests for use, and access to materials (including Internet access). In many settings, the duties of the curator and the **archivist** overlap.

DAT (Digital audio tape). (Recording technology) Digital recording format popular in the 1990s. It is rarely used now and should never be used for preservation.

data migration. *See* **migrate**.

database. (Information technology) A collection of related data that is organized so that its contents can easily be accessed, managed, and updated. Library catalogs are relational databases. Databases are organized by fields, records, and files. A field is a single piece of information; a record is a group of related fields pertaining to a single entity; and a file is a collection of records. For example, a telephone book is analogous to a file. It contains a list of records, each of which consists of three fields: name, address, and telephone number.

DCHI. *See* **Digital Cultural Heritage Initiative**.

deed of gift. (Law) An agreement transferring title to property without compensation. Most oral histories are passed from the interviewer or narrator to the archive through this document. *See also* **contract**.

defamation. (Law) A false statement of fact printed or broadcast about a person, which tends to injure that person's interest. When the words are printed, the offense is *libel*; when the words are spoken, the offense is *slander*.

description. (Archives) A term used in archival practice for all the steps that provide **intellectual control** over the item—cataloging, finding aids, indexing. The more detailed the description, the easier it is for researchers to find it.

desktop microphone. *See* **clip-on/desktop microphone**.

digital. (Recording technology) A process that captures and stores sound by taking samples of a sound wave, rather than the continuous signal. Digital is becoming the preferred method for recording sound, because of its higher quality and the ease of manipulating sound files. *See also* **analog**.

digital audio tape. *See* **DAT**.

Digital Cultural Heritage Initiative (DCHI). (Information technology) A program engaged in using digital technology to develop a product, such as an online exhibition, or sound archive, for the purpose of preserving and making available our cultural heritage.

digital rights management (DRM). (Information technology) An umbrella term to describe the technologies that control and monitor digital content on the Internet. Information may be monitored for reasons of copyright or intellectual property protection, confidentiality, or regulatory compliance. DRM will become an increasing issue for curators as oral history collections are entered into digital archives or on the Internet.

digital storytelling. (Oral history) A popular method for recording and preserving personal or family stories using multimedia.

digital video. (Recording technology) A method for recording moving images. Can be recorded and stored on tapes or discs. Do not confuse with **DV**, which is a special kind of digital video. *See also* **video**.

digitization. (Preservation) The act of transferring a sound recording from analog (continuous wave) format to digital (samples of the sound wave converted to bits and bytes).

directional/omnidirectional microphone. (Recording technology) A directional microphone picks up sound from a certain direction. The most common type is cardioid, which picks up sound in a heart-shaped field, designed to prevent feedback. An omnidirectional microphone picks up sound from any direction.

document. (Information technology) A generic term to describe a *unit of information* in either the physical or virtual world. A document can be a book, a broadside, or an oral history transcript or recording in the physical world. In the virtual world the terms *document* and *file* are used interchangeably—as in a sound file, an image file, or a text document. *See also* **file**.

DRM. *See* **digital rights management**.

Dublin Core. (Cataloging) A **metadata** scheme designed by librarians to describe electronic resources (websites) in library catalogs.

DV. (Recording technology) A digital format for recording moving images. *See also* **digital video**, **video**, **DVD**.

DVD. (Recording technology) An optical disc used for storing digital information. DVDs hold much more information than CDs but less

Disc	Type	Storage	Used for
DVD-ROM, DVD-Video, DVD-Audio	Read only	Varies; 5-17 GB	Commercial uses: movies, games, computer programs
DVD-R	Record once	4-5GB	Audio and video recording and editing
DVD-RW	Rewritable	4-5GB	Not recommended for preservation

is known about their preservation qualities. DVDs look like CDs but behave differently. (Originally Digital Video Disc, then Digital Versatile Disc, currently doesn't stand for anything at all.) See table above. *See also* **CD**.

dynamic/condenser microphone. (Recording technology) A dynamic microphone does not need separate power to operate. A condenser microphone requires power, usually from a battery or **phantom power**. Dynamic microphones are more durable; condenser microphones are more sensitive. *See also* **microphone**.

EAD (Encoded Archival Description). (Information technology) A metadata scheme designed to create digital finding aids for archival materials. *See also* **metadata**.

external microphone. (Recording technology) A **microphone** that is separate from the recording machine.

fair use doctrine. (Law) A provision in copyright law that allows the limited use of copyrighted materials for educational purposes.

field. (Information technology) A component in a database which is defined to contain certain characteristics for all the data entered into it. *See also* **database**.

file. (Information technology) A unit of related data, sometimes referred to as a document. Examples: a text document, a spreadsheet, an image, or an audio file. *See also* **document**.

file format. (Information technology) A fuzzy term used to describe various categories and distinctions in information technology. In this book I use the term to describe protocols that can be understood by certain computer programs, e.g., .xcl by Excel, .doc by Microsoft word, .wam by Windows Media. It is important to make the distinction between proprietary formats, which can only be understood by particular commercial programs, and open source formats, which can be understood universally.

finding aid. (Archives) The descriptive tool used by archivists to keep track of physical and intellectual content of archival materials. Finding aids generally have a hierarchical design, beginning with a collection-level description, followed by a series within the collection, and finally item-level descriptions within each series.

Flash memory. (Recording technology) A solid-state memory chip that can retain data even after the recording device is turned off.

flat database. *See* **database**.

format. *See* **file format**.

FRBR (Functional Requirements for Bibliographic Records). (Cataloging) An international protocol for describing bibliographic resources, as an alternative to AACR. *See also* **Anglo American Cataloging Rules**, **RDA**.

gift. (Law) Voluntary transfer of property without getting anything in return. Oral histories are generally transferred to repositories as gifts.

hyperlink. (Information technology) A reference to related material on the same web page or on a different website. Hyperlinks allow users to navigate around the World Wide Web to find the information they need quickly by clicking on the highlighted term. Hyperlinks are similar to **cross references** in a library catalog.

index. (Cataloging) An alphabetical list of topics or names with references to pages or sections to a larger document. An index is a tool for better access within a document.

index term. (Cataloging) A field within a database, such as a library catalog, defined as searchable. Examples of index terms in a catalog record for an oral history are the narrator's name, the interviewer's name, the topic of the interview, and the name of the oral history project. *See also* **access point**.

informant. *See* **narrator**.

informed consent. (Law) An agreement to do something or allow something to happen, made with complete knowledge of all relevant facts, such as the risks involved or any available alternatives. For example, the narrator should be completely informed of all the potential uses of his interview.

intellectual control. (Archives) A method for providing documentation for an archival collection—such as making a finding aid or catalog record—so that the *content* of the collection can easily be accessed and maintained. *See also* **bibliographic control**.

intellectual property. (Law) The area of law that regulates the ownership and use of creative works, including patent, copyright, and trademark. *See also* **copyright**.

Internet. (Information technology) A giant network of computers—billions of them—which serves as infrastructure for the World Wide Web, email, FTP, and other kinds of data exchange.

interview. (Oral history) A structured question-and-answer session between a **narrator** and **interviewer** characterized by well-focused, open-ended, neutral questions. The interview is the basis for all oral history. *See also* **oral history**.

interviewee. *See* **narrator**.

interviewer. (Oral history) The person who asks questions and guides the structure of an interview. The interviewer is responsible for the *structure* of the interview and the narrator is responsible for the *content*.

invasion of privacy. (Law) The law protects us from invasion of privacy based on four actions. The action most relevant to oral history is *public disclosure of intimate private facts*.

inventory. (Archives) A list of the documents within a repository, and the attributes of each. Can also refer to the act of creating this list.

item. (Archives) An item is the smallest archival unit or **document** (e.g., a letter, photograph, interview disc).

item level record. (Cataloging) As contrasted to a **collection level record**, this catalog record describes each oral history separately. This method of cataloging provides much more detail.

lavaliere microphone. *See* **clip-on/desktop microphone**.

legal consent form. (Law) A legal agreement between the narrator and the interviewer which clarifies the nature of the interview relationship. It should include the following points: intent to conduct the interview, delivery and acceptance of the interview, copyright assignment, the narrator's rights to future use, and any restrictions on the content of the interview.

libel. *See* **defamation**.

license. (Law) The transfer of rights from the original holder to another party, generally for a specific use, duration, and territory. This is a common alternative to ownership in the digital world, for example, an e-book is *licensed* to a user, whereas a print book is *owned* by a library, and *borrowed* by a user. *See also* **ownership**.

life expectancy. (Archives) The length of time that an item is expected to remain intact and useful when kept in a typical office environment (70°F/21°C and 50% RH). This term is gaining favor over the older term **archival quality**, because it specifies measurements of longevity.

life history. (Oral history) An oral history that emphasizes the entire span of a person's life, as opposed to a **topical history**, which emphasizes many people's experience around a single topic.

link. *See* **hyperlink**, **cross reference**.

loss of lubricant (LoL). (Preservation) A chemical condition that causes audiocassette tapes to deteriorate. *See also* **Sticky Shed Syndrome**.

magnetic tape. (Recording technology) A tape coated with a magnetic material which stores information as electromagnetic signals. Magnetic tape is the most common medium for oral histories in archives today, but as a recording medium, it is being phased out.

magneto-optical (MO). (Recording technology). A type of data storage that combines magnetic and optical technologies. For example, some minidiscs are magneto-optical.

management system. (Management) A database system for keeping records for collections, projects, or online content. The system usually tracks tasks and objectives, with links to an inventory of materials processed, and people involved. A management system can be set up locally using a database or spreadsheet, or can be purchased as a package. The functions of management systems described below overlap, but commercial products come under one of these names, and emphasize certain management functions over others. See table below.

MARC format (Machine-Readable Cataloging). (Cataloging) A data exchange standard developed by the Library of Congress and, until recently, accepted worldwide as the standard for library cataloging.

MD. *See* **minidisc**.

media independent. (Information technology) Digital files that are not dependent on a particular recording medium. Media-independent digital content is stored and can be transported on media, e.g., CD-R, portable hard disk, and data tape, but this use of media is incidental to the content.

metadata. (Information technology) Data about data. Metadata provides all kinds of information about how a computer should handle the data behind the scenes. Metadata is becoming increasingly important as the world moves to a digital environment for information storage, retrieval, and delivery. (See table on p. 131.)

METS (Metadata Encoding and Transmission Standard). (Information technology) A standard, maintained by the Library of Congress, for encoding various kinds of metadata to describe digital files. METS coordinates the schema designed for particular disciplines, such as **EAD** or TEI.

microphone. (Recording technology) A device that converts sound to electrical signals, usually for amplification. Though microphones occur inside recorders, **external microphones** provide higher quality sound and should be used for oral history interviews. A variety of microphones are available with different attributes. *See also* **directional/omnidirectional microphone**, **dynamic/condenser microphone**, **stereophonic/monophonic microphone**, **clip-on/desk-top microphone**.

Common Management Systems for Oral History Curators

Content management	Almost always refers to *digital content*. Controls the authoring, editing, updating, and digital rights management.
Collection management	Used for managing a project or archive. Tracks inventory, physical condition, availability, legal papers.
Project management	Tracks and connects all the tasks and attributes of a project – timeframe, people involved, who does what, budgeting, and how it all gets accomplished.

Kinds of Metadata	
Descriptive	Describes the intellectual content
Administrative	Information about ownership, restrictions, etc.
Structural	Describes the relationships between multiple digital files, such as the order of audio files that form a series
Technical	Technical features such as file type, bit depth, and sample rate

migrate. (Preservation) To move analog or digital data from one computer storage system to another. *See also* **refresh**, **reformat**.

minidisc (MD). (Recording technology) A digital recording medium popular with oral historians in the 1990s because of its convenient size and affordability. However, a recording from the minidisc can't be directly transferred to a computer for reformatting or editing. A newer version, called Hi-MD, was introduced in 2004 to solve the problem.

mini-DV. *See* **DV**.

MO. *See* **magneto-optical**.

monophonic microphone. *See* **stereophonic/ monophonic microphone.**

narrator. (Oral history) The person being interviewed—whose story will be narrated through the interview. *See also* **interviewer**.

obsolescence. (Preservation) The loss of value or usefulness of an object even though it functions well. This can be due to outmoded equipment, inability to buy parts, newer technology, or a change in public taste.

OCLC (Online Computer Library Center). (Cataloging) An international **bibliographic utility** hosting the world's largest catalog for books, artifacts, sound and visual recordings, and more. The public interface for OCLC is WorldCat, and is available to users in most libraries around the world.

online catalog. *See* **OPAC**.

OPAC (Online Public Access Catalog). (Cataloging) A computerized library catalog running on a relational database.

omnidirectional microphone. *See* **directional/ omnidirectional microphone**.

open-reel tape. (Recording technology) Tape supplied on its own reel and not contained in a cartridge or cassette. Open-reel tape was popular for recording oral histories in the 1940s and 1950s, and is still prevalent in archives.

open source. (Information technology) A computer program's source code or file format that is open and available to the world.

optical media. (Recording technology, Preservation) Media, such as CD and DVD, that use laser technology for digital data storage and retrieval. Different kinds of optical discs have different features. *See also* **magnetic tape**, **solid state**.

oral history. 1. The documentation of recent history by means of a recorded, structured interview. 2. The discipline that has grown up around this methodology. 3. A "package" which includes an **interview** or series of interviews related by content, often with transcript and supporting materials, made available for public use.

oral tradition. (Oral history) A community's cultural and historical background preserved and passed on from one generation to the next in spoken stories and song, as distinct from a written tradition.

original order. (Archives) An archival principle referring to the importance of keeping archival papers together and in the same order as they were arranged by the creator, in order to preserve the context. This principle is also referred to as *respect des fonds*. *See also* **provenance**.

orphaned documents. (Archives) Documents in an archive that, for whatever reason, can't be made available to the public. Oral histories are often orphaned because the proper legal consent form is missing, or because the equipment for listening to the interview is obsolete or unavailable.

outcome. (Management) Specific goals that should result from a task. This concept is important in project design and grant writing.

outsource. (Management) To contract with an independent agency for a task. A choice to outsource depends on the archive's collection, goals, and resources. Some pros and cons are listed in the table below.

phased preservation. (Preservation) An approach to preservation that emphasizes activities to protect the entire holdings of a repository, rather than concentrating solely on evaluating and treating individual items. Such an approach includes, but is not limited to, preservation planning and surveys to establish priorities, disaster planning, controlling storage environment, performing holdings maintenance, and selective treatment of materials.

preservation. (Preservation) Actions taken to stabilize and protect documents and artifacts from deteriorating, as well as retrospectively treating or restoring damaged documents. Preservation also includes the transfer of information to another medium.

Outsourcing	In-House
You pay only for the job done, not for employees or equipment.	Staff can learn tasks and perform them as they go.
Usually high-quality work and good turnaround time.	Staff exercise more control over project and can adjust specifications as you work.
Usually contractor is expert in the field.	Easier to customize project to fit archive's needs.
Contractor absorbs cost of technology obsolescence, failure, downtime, etc.	Requires initial and ongoing financial investment.
Archive loses some control of technical details.	Requires initial and ongoing equipment purchase.
Relationship with contractor and vendor requires technical specifications upfront, and plan for quality control.	Staff expertise not always available.
Original recordings must leave archive.	Existing staff must be given sufficient time to do the job. May take time away from other tasks.
Potential for misunderstanding on technical specifications, turnaround time, or local practices.	Institution must absorb costs of computer downtime, equipment failure, staff training, etc.
	Responsible for standards and best practices.

ownership. (Law) The person or legal entity that holds physical ownership of the item, along with all the accompanying rights and responsibilities. *See also* **license**.

phantom power. (Recording technology) A method of providing power to condenser microphones, by tapping into the power supply of the recording device it is attached to.

preservation master. (Preservation) The first copy made from a recorded interview. The original recording should be permanently stored in another location, and subsequent copies should be made from the preservation master.

primary source. (Oral history) First-hand information with no interpretation between the document and the researcher. An oral history is a primary resource, as are diaries and correspondence. *See also* **secondary source**.

print through. (Preservation) A condition of magnetic tape deterioration when the information on one section of the magnetic tape bleeds through onto the next layer of tape on the spool. Print through can be avoided by rewinding the tape periodically. *See also* **Sticky Shed Syndrome**.

processing. (Archives) The organization, description, and arrangement of documents to make them available for public use.

program. *See* **project**.

project/program. (Management) A project has a specific goal and ending date; a program is ongoing. A program usually has ongoing funding and is often part of a larger institution, such as a library or university. Programs often support individual projects.

project management system. *See* **management system**.

project manager. (Management) The person responsible for the overall administration of a project. For an oral history project, duties include project design; fundraising and budgeting; purchasing and maintaining recording equipment; keeping records; selecting and training interviewers; overseeing transcription, cataloging and processing; **rights management**; and meeting deadlines. In practice, an oral history project manager's tasks often overlap with those of the **curator** or **archivist**.

proprietary format. *See* **format**.

proprietary software. (Information technology) A computer program where the creator controls the source code. *See also* **open source**.

provenance. (Archives) The relationships between the records that come into an archive and their original owners. *See also* **original order**, **arrangement**.

public domain. (Law) A creative work that is not subject to the copyright laws and may be used without permission of the creator or former rights holder. The work could either be ex-

pressly created for the public domain, or it could be in the public domain because the copyright limitation has expired. *See also* **copyright**.

RAID (Redundant array of independent discs). (Information technology) A method for storing large quantities of data on servers with minimal risk of losing the data.

RDA (Resource Description and Access). (Cataloging) A new standard, scheduled to supersede AACR, which will better meet the needs of cataloging in a digital environment.

record. 1. (Archives) Any document which supports a function, such as "keeping records on the project." 2. (Archives) A document created or received by an agency, organization, or individual, in pursuance of legal obligations or business transactions. 3. (Information technology) An element in the hierarchical structure of a **database**. A record contains related *fields*, and is contained in a *file*.

recording medium (pl. **media**). (Recording technology) The physical carrier for recording or storing information, such as disc, tape, CD, CD-ROM. Though there is technically a difference between recording medium, storage medium, and preservation medium, they are commonly used interchangeably.

recording unit. (Recording technology) A customized "kit" for audio or video recording equipment. Can include recorder, microphone, cables, and batteries.

reel-to-reel tape. *See* **open-reel tape**.

refresh. (Preservation) To make an exact copy of data in a newer medium of the same kind (e.g., from an old cassette to a newer one) for preservation. *See also* **reformat**, **migrate**.

reformat. (Preservation) To make a copy with a structure, format, or recording medium different from the original, in order to preserve the content. *See also* **refresh**, **migrate**.

release form. *See* **legal consent form**.

relational database. *See* **database**.

relative humidity. (Archives) The amount of moisture in the air, expressed as a percent of the maximum moisture air can hold at a given temperature.

repository. (Archives) The permanent *physical* home for historic documents. *See also* **archives**.

Resource Description and Access. *See* **RDA**.

respect des fonds. *See* **original order**.

restrictions. (Law) Limitation imposed by the narrator to legally restrict access to all or part of the interview content, for a limited time or permanently. Though such restrictions are discouraged by both interviewers and curators, they are sometimes unavoidable.

rights management. (Archives) The collection of duties connected to the intellectual property rights of oral histories. Rights management can include tracking restrictions, copyright, and permission to use.

sampling rate. (Recording technology) The number of samples from a sound wave that the computer takes to make a digital file. The larger the sample, the higher the quality and the closer the digital representation represents the original sound.

scalability. (Management) A criterion used to determine whether a procedure can be adapted to a much larger or much smaller situation.

search engine. (Information technology) A computer program designed to help users find information on the World Wide Web, or within a particular database. Google is the most common search engine.

secondary source. (Oral history) Interpretive work based on the evidence contained in **primary sources**.

server. (Information technology) A computer that delivers a "service" to other computers in a network. Common servers are file (data) servers, print servers, and mail servers.

slander. *See* **defamation**.

solid state. (Recording technology) A storage device that uses a computer chip, with no moving parts. Newer recording units use solid-state technology. *See also* **magnetic tape**, **optical media**.

spreadsheet. (Information technology) A table consisting of cells arranged in rows and columns, where the contents of each cell is defined in relation to the others. The relationships between cells are defined by the user as formulas. A computer program such as Excel is needed to read and manipulate the data in a spreadsheet.

stereophonic/monophonic microphone. (Recording technology) A stereophonic microphone records sound from various sources on different channels. A monophonic microphone records all sounds on a single channel. Stereo microphones can also record as mono, which is usually sufficient for oral history interviews.

Sticky Shed Syndrome. (Preservation) Audiotape deterioration characterized by gummy deposits on tape path guides and heads after a sticky tape has been played. Appears most commonly on reel-to-reel tapes. *See also* **loss of lubricant**.

streaming audio. (Information technology) A method of transferring sound so it can be processed in a steady and continuous stream. This method should be used for oral histories made available over the Internet.

structure. (Information technology) Refers to physical qualities of a document or file, such as the size, format, or medium. The distinction between structure and **content** is an important one for cataloging and preservation management.

subject headings. (Cataloging) Descriptive terms pertaining to the item cataloged, based on a **controlled vocabulary**.

summary. (Oral history) A condensation of an interview, highlighting the key points. A summary can range from a paragraph to a few pages, depending on the purpose. Summaries are useful for curators evaluating a collection, for catalogers, for researchers, and for websites or printed catalogs.

syndetic structures. (Cataloging) The structure of related terms that provide access points in catalog records, such as *see* and *see also* terms, or *broader* and *narrower* terms. Understanding syndetic structures is important for creating meaningful access points in a catalog. This glossary uses *see* and *see also* elements of syndetic structures.

tape log. (Oral history) An annotated list of topics covered in the interview, indexed at timed intervals. A tape log is a useful tool for researchers to find sections on an audiotape, but is less useful if the sound is edited, rearranged, or transferred to another medium.

thesaurus. (Cataloging) A list of terms and concepts, usually dealing with a specific discipline, that provides a standardized vocabulary to use in searching a database. *See also* **authority control, controlled vocabulary**.

topical history. (Oral history) A series of interviews with a variety of people who witnessed or experienced a particular topic or event. *See also* **life history**.

transcript. (Oral history) A verbatim printed version of the spoken word.

uncompressed. *See* **compressed/uncompressed data**.

URL (Uniform Resource Locator). (Information technology) A unique address to a web page. URLs have this or a similar format: http://www.google.com

user copy. (Oral history) Third-generation copy of audio recording, made for public use. *See also* **preservation master.**

VHS (Video Home System, originally **Vertical Helical Scan)**. (Recording technology) An analog system for recording moving images—standard for consumer video recording until digital video became practical. *See also* **video**.

video. (Recording technology) A method of capturing moving images using film, tape, electronic signals, or digital media. *See also* **VHS, DV, digital video**.

visual history. (Oral history) A recorded interview using video instead of audio.

website. (Information technology) A set of related web pages, usually including a homepage, that are organized to present a person, organization, or idea. Web pages can include text, graphics, hyperlinks, a search engine, sound, and video.

World Cat. *See* **OCLC**.

World Wide Web. (Information technology) A network of web pages on the **Internet**, available via a **browser** and a unique address or **URL**, most easily found through a **search engine**. The number of web pages is estimated to be in the billions, and growing daily. The World Wide Web is rapidly becoming a universal point for information exchange and delivery.

APPENDIX D

RESOURCES

This list is also available online at http://www.nancymackay.net/curating/resources.htm.

ORAL HISTORY

Baum, Willa K. *Oral history for the local historical society.* 3rd ed. (AltaMira Press, 1995).

Charlton, Thomas L., Lois E. Myers, and M. Rebecca Sharpless, eds. *Handbook of oral history.* (AltaMira Press, 2006).

Dunaway, David K., and Willa K. Baum, eds. *Oral history: an interdisciplinary anthology.* 2nd ed. (AltaMira Press, 1996).

Frisch, Michael. *A shared authority: essays on the craft and meaning of oral history and public history.* (State University of New York Press, 1990).

H-NET (Online community). Interdisciplinary community of scholars and educators in the humanities and social sciences. Supports online discussion groups in specialized areas, including the ones mentioned below. http://www.h-net.org.

H-ORALHIST (Online discussion group). Moderated H-Net discussion group serves the oral history community. Subscription information and archives at http://www.h-net.org/~oralhist.

H-PUBLIC (Online discussion group). Moderated H-Net discussion group for public history. Subscription information and archives at http://www.h-net.org/~public.

Lanman, Barry A., and Laura M. Wending, eds. *Preparing the next generation of oral historians: an anthology of oral history education.* (AltaMira Press, 2006).

Linehan, Andy, ed. *Aural history: essays on recorded sound.* (British Library, National Sound Archive, 2001). Book plus CD. Published on the occasion International Association of Sound and Audiovisual Archives Conference.

Oral History Association. *Evaluation guidelines.* http://www.dickinson.edu/oha/pub_eg.html.

Perks, Robert, and Alistair Thomson, eds. *The oral history reader.* 2nd ed. (Routledge, 2006).

Portelli, Alessandro. *The battle of Valle Giulia: oral history and the art of dialogue.* (University of Wisconsin Press, 1997).

——. *The death of Luigi Trastulli and other stories: form and meaning in oral history.* (State University of New York Press, 1991).

——. *The order has been carried out: history, memory and meaning of a Nazi massacre in Rome.* (Palgrave Macmillan, 2003).

Ritchie, Donald A. *Doing oral history: a practical guide.* 2nd ed. (Oxford University Press, 2003).

Schneider, William. *So they understand: cultural issues in oral history.* (Utah State University Press, 2002).

Sommer, Barbara W., and Mary Kay Quinlan. *The oral history manual.* (AltaMira Press, 2002).

Thompson, Paul. *The voice of the past: oral history.* 3rd ed. (Oxford University Press, 2000).

Whitman, Glenn. *Dialogue with the past: engaging students & meeting standards through oral history.* (AltaMira Press, 2004).

Yow, Valerie Raleigh. *Recording oral history: a guide for the humanities and social sciences.* 2nd ed. (AltaMira Press, 2005).

ARCHIVES ADMINISTRATION

Archives and Archivists Listserv (Online discussion group). Unmoderated, high-volume forum for archivists. Archives available. Subscribe at http://listserv.muohio.edu/archives/archives.html.

ARMA International and Society of American Archivists. *Sample forms for archival and records management programs.* (ARMA, SAA, 2002). Forms in electronic format can be copied from accompanying CD.

Bradsher, James Gregory. *Managing archives and archival institutions.* (University of Chicago Press, 1991).

Carmicheal, David W. *Organizing archival records: a practical method of arrangement & description for small archives.* 2nd ed. (AltaMira Press, 2005).

Danielson, Virginia, Elizabeth Cohen, and Anthony Seeger. *Folk heritage collections in crisis.* (CLIR, 2001). Papers from a 2000 conference on the condition of heritage collections. http://www.clir.org/pubs/reports/pub96/contents.html.

Farrington, Jim. *Audio and video equipment basics for libraries.* (Scarecrow Press, 2006).

Fox, Michael J., Peter Wilkerson, and Suzanne Warren. *Introduction to archival organization and description: access to cultural heritage.* (Getty Information Institute, 1999). http://www.getty.edu/research/conducting_research/standards/introarchives.

NINCH guide to good practice in the digital representation and management of cultural heritage materials. (NINCH, 2002). http://www.nyu.edu/its/humanities/ninchguide.

Hunter, Gregory S. *Developing and maintaining practical archives: a how-to-do-it manual.* 2nd ed. (Neal-Schuman, 2003).

International Council on Archives. *General International Standard Archival Description (ISAD(G)).* 2nd ed. (International Council on Archives, 2000). http://www.ica.org/biblio/cds/isad_g_2e.pdf.

Kurtz, Michael. *Managing archival and manuscript repositories.* (Society of American Archivists, 2004).

Pearce-Moses, Richard. *Glossary of archival and records terminology.* (Society of American Archivists, 2005). http://www.archivists.org/glossary.

Roe, Kathleen D. *Arranging & describing archives & manuscripts.* (Society of American Archivists, 2005). Supersedes Frederic Miller's *Arranging and describing archives and manuscripts* (1990).

Society of American Archivists. *Describing archives: a content standard (DACS).* (Society of American Archivists, 2004.) Revised standard for archival description. Supersedes Steven Hensen's *Archives, personal papers and manuscripts* (1989).

———. *A guide to deeds of gift.* (Society of American Archivists, 1998). http://www.archivists.org/publications/deed_of_gift.asp.

Stielow, Frederick J. *The management of oral history sound archives.* (Greenwood Press, 1986).

Swain, Ellen D. "Oral history in the archives: its documentary role in the twenty-first century," *American Archivist* 66 (Spring/Summer 2003): 139–158.

Walch, Victoria Irons, comp. *Standards for archival description: a handbook.* (Society of American Archivists, 1994). Online version by Stephen Miller. http://www.archivists.org/catalog/stds99/index.html.

Ward, Alan. *A manual of sound archive administration.* (Gower Publishing Company, 1990).

Wilsted, Thomas, and William Nolte. *Managing archival and manuscript repositories.* (Society of American Archivists, 1991).

Yakel, Elizabeth. *Starting an archives.* (Society of American Archivists, Scarecrow Press, 1994).

LEGAL & ETHICAL ISSUES

Benedict, Karen. *Ethics and the archival profession: introduction and case studies.* (Society of American Archivists, 2003). Forty case studies covering all aspects of archival management.

Brown, Michael F. "Can culture be copyrighted?" *Current Anthropology* 39, 2 (April 1998): 193–222.

Copyright Resources Project: working with copyrighted materials in a digital environment (University of California Art Museum & Pacific Film Archive, 2005). http://www.bampfa.berkeley.edu/pfa_library/copyright_project.

Digital Millennium Copyright Act (DMCA). http://www.copyright.gov/legislation/dmca.pdf. Government summary of the legislation. For a summary and interpretation from the UCLA Institute for Cyberspace Law and Policy, see http://www.gseis.ucla.edu/iclp/dmca1.htm.

Fair Use in the Electronic Age, compiled by American Association of Law Libraries, American Library Association, Association of Academic Health Sciences Library Directors, Association of Research Libraries, Medical Library Association, and Special Libraries Association. http://www.arl.org/info/frn/copy/fairuse.html.

Lipinski, Thomas A., ed. *Libraries, museums and archives: legal issues and ethical challenges in the new Information Age.* (Scarecrow Press, 2002).

Neuenschwander, John A. *Oral history and the law.* 3rd ed. (Oral History Association, 2002). Acknowledged authority among oral historians for legal issues in oral history.

Padfield, Tim. *Copyright for archivists and users of archives.* 2nd ed. (Facet, 2004). Copyright issues in the United Kingdom.

Russell, Carrie. *Complete copyright: an everyday guide for librarians.* (American Library Association, 2004).

Schneider, William. *So they understand: cultural issues in oral history.* (Utah State University Press, 2002). Ethical issues in oral history.

Society of American Archivists. *A guide to deeds of gift.* (Society of American Archivists, 1998). http://www.archivists.org/publications/deed_of_gift.asp.

Stim, Richard. *Getting permission: how to license & clear copyrighted materials online & off.* (Nolo Press, 2004).

United States Copyright Office. *Report on orphan works.* (United States Copyright Office, Library of Congress, 2006). http://www.copyright.gov/orphan/orphan-report-full.pdf.

University of Texas. *Fair use of copyrighted works.* Sample interpretation of fair use. http://www.utsystem.edu/OGC/intellectualProperty/copypol2.htm.

Professional Ethical Standards

Alaska Native Knowledge Network. *Guidelines for respecting cultural knowledge.* Adopted 2000. http://www.ankn.uaf.edu/publications/knowledge.html.

American Anthropological Association. *Statements on ethics.* Rev. 1986. http://www.aaanet.org/stmts/ethstmnt.htm.

American Association for State and Local History. *Statement of professional standards and ethics.* Rev. 2002. http://www.aaslh.org/ethics.htm.

American Association of Museums. *Code of ethics for museums.* Rev. 2000. http://www.aam-us.org/museumresources/ethics/coe.cfm.

American Historical Association. *Statement on standards of professional conduct.* Rev. 2005. http://www.historians.org/pubs/Free/ProfessionalStandards.cfm.

American Library Association. *Code of ethics.* http://www.ala.org/ala/oif/statementspols/codeofethics/codeethics.htm.

Oral History Association. *Evaluation Guidelines.* Rev. 2000. http://omega.dickinson.edu/organizations/oha/pub_eg.html.

Society of American Archivists. *Code of ethics for archivists*. Rev. 2005. http://www.archivists.org/governance/handbook/app_ethics.asp.

RECORDING TECHNOLOGY

AMIL-L: Online forum for moving image archivists. Subscription information and archives at http://www.amianet.org/amial/amial.html.

ARSC recorded round discussion list. Unmoderated discussion list for sound recording discussions at all levels. Subscription information at http://www.arsc-audio.org/arsclist.html.

Bennett, Hugh. *Understanding CD-R and CD-RW: physical, logical and file system standards*. (Optical Storage Technology Association, 2003). http://www.osta.org/technology/pdf/cdr_cdrw.pdf.

DAT-Heads: Digital Audio Tape. Online discussion group for digital audio tape. http://www.solorb.com/dat-heads.

Hess, Richard. *Media formats and resources*. Demystifies recording formats. http://richardhess.com/notes/formats.

Historical Voices. *Oral history tutorial: audio technology*. (MATRIX [Michigan State University], 2002). http://www.historicalvoices.org/oralhistory/audio-tech.html.

Kovolos, Andy. *Audio field recording equipment guide*. (Vermont Folklife Center, frequent updates). The latest information on audio technology specifically for oral historians. http://www.vermontfolklifecenter.org/res_audioequip.htm.

Magnetic Reference Laboratory. *MRL homepage*. (Magnetic Reference Laboratory, frequently updated). Everything about magnetic tape. http://home.flash.net/~mrltapes.

Minidisc.org. Everything about minidiscs. http://www.minidisc.org.

Morton, David L. *History of sound recording technology*. (2003). http://www.recording-history.org.

————. *Sound recording: the life story of a technology*. (Johns Hopkins University, 2006).

ProAction Media. *Online glossary of CD/DVD terms*. (ProAction Media, 2005). http://www.proactionmedia.com/cd_dvd_glossary.htm.

Robbins, Ryan. *The Holy Grail of digital recording*. (Tape Transcription Center, n.d.). http://www.ttctranscriptions.com/DigitalRecordingHolyGrail.html.

Schoenherr, Steve. *Recording technology history*. (2005). Timeline for recording technology. http://history.sandiego.edu/gen/recording/notes.html.

Schouhamer Immink, Kees A. "The compact disc story." *Journal of Audio Engineering Society* 46, 5 (May 1998). http://www.exp-math.uni-essen.de/~immink/pdf/cdstory.pdf.

Smolian, Steve. *SoundSaver.com: CDs from old recordings*. (SoundSaver.com, frequently updated). Overview of older recording technology. http://soundsaver.com.

Tape Transcription Center. *Digital recording: here to stay*. (Tape Transcription Center, 2006). http://www.ttctranscriptions.com/Digitalvsanalog.html.

Taylor, Jim. *DVD demystified*. 3rd ed. (McGraw-Hill, 2006). A lot of information on accompanying website: http://www.dvddemystified.com.

Transom.org. (Atlantic Public Media, frequently updated). Easy to understand tips on recording technology. http://www.transom.org/tools.

UCSC Electronic Music Studios. *EMS equipment documents*. (University of California, Santa Cruz, Music Dept., content frequently updated). Technical articles on recording technology, with illustrations. http://arts.ucsc.edu/ems/music/equipment/equipment.html.

Wikipedia has a variety of articles with helpful links on recording technology. http://en.wikipedia.org.

TRANSCRIBING

Baum, Willa K. *Transcribing and editing oral history.* (AltaMira Press, 1995).

Frisch, Michael. "Oral history and the digital revolution: toward a post-documentary sensibility." In *The oral history reader.* 2nd ed., Robert Perks and Alistair Thomson, eds. (Routledge, 2006). A case for alternatives to transcribing.

Klemmer, Scott R., et al. "Books with voices: paper transcripts as a physical interface to oral histories." In *Proceedings of the SIGCHI conference on human factors in computer systems,* 2003. 89–96.

Powers, Willow Roberts. *Transcription techniques for the spoken word.* (AltaMira Press, 2005).

University of Chicago Press. *Chicago manual of style.* 15th ed. (University of Chicago Press, 2003). Accepted standard among oral historians for usage, editing, and proofreading.

Wilmsen, Carl. "For the record: editing and the production of meaning in oral history." *Oral history review* 28, 1 (Winter 2001).

Transcription Software

Express-scribe transcription playback software. (NCH Swift Sound). Free software for transcribing from digital files. http://www.nch.com.au/scribe.

Start-stop dictation and transcription systems. (HTH Engineering). Software for transcribing from digital files. http://www.startstop.com.

Transcribing & Editing Guides

Minnesota Historical Society Oral History Office. *Transcribing, editing and processing oral histories.* (Oral History Association of Minnesota, 1996). http://www.oham.org/how/transcribe.html.

Baylor University Institute for Oral History. *Style guide: a quick guide for editing oral memoirs.* Rev. 2005. http://www.baylor.edu/oral%5Fhistory/index.php?id=23607.

CATALOGING

American Library Association. *Anglo-American Cataloging Rules.* 2nd ed. (American Library Association, 2002). Published loose-leaf, with quarterly updates. Standard for bibliographic description and analysis for libraries since the 1960s, however catalogers are questioning its relevancy, and alternative standards are being explored.

AUTOCAT (Online discussion group). A semi-moderated list serving the international cataloging community. Subscription information and searchable archives available at http://ublib.buffalo.edu/libraries/units/cts/autocat.

Calhoun, Karen. *The changing nature of the catalog and its integration with other discovery tools.* Final report. (Library of Congress, 2006). This study, commissioned by the Library of Congress, assesses the effectiveness of current library catalogs, and makes recommendations for a newer model to reflect the information needs of 21st century users. http://www.loc.gov/catdir/calhoun-report-final.pdf.

Describing archives: a content standard (DACS). (Society of American Archivists, 2004). Revised standard for archival description adapted by U.S. archives, supersedes *Archives, personal papers and manuscripts* (1989).

IASA Cataloging rules: a manual for the description of sound recordings and related audiovisual media. Compiled and edited by the IASA Editorial Group convened by Mary Miliano. (Stockholm: IASAA, 1999). International standard for cataloging sound recordings.

Library of Congress. *MARC Standards.* Official website for MARC, the internationally recognized bibliographic encoding standard. http://www.loc.gov/marc.

Matters, Marion. *Oral history cataloging manual.* (Society of American Archivists, 1995). Designed for library catalogers. Many examples in MARC format, applying AACRII rules.

OCLC. *Bibliographic formats and standards.* MARC format description, as interpreted by

OCLC. http://www.oclc.org/bibformats/default.htm.

OLAC: online audiovisual catalogers. Internet and AV Media catalogers network, including an online discussion group. http://ublib.buffalo.edu/libraries/units/cts/olac.

Plassard, Marie-France, ed. *Functional requirements for bibliographic records: final report. (FRBR).* (Saar, 1998). http://www.ifla.org/VII/s13/frbr/frbr.pdf

Program for cooperative cataloging. (Library of Congress). An international cooperative effort to expand access to library collections. http://www.loc.gov/catdir/pcc.

Resources Description Framework (maintained by W3C). A portal, frequently updated, for RDF development, an area that will increasingly involve traditional catalogers. http://www.w3.org/RDF.

Tillett, Barbara. *What is FRBR? a conceptual model for the bibliographic universe.* (Library of Congress, Cataloging Distribution Service, 2004). http://www.loc.gov/cds/FRBR.html.

Walch, Victoria Irons, comp. *Standards for archival description: a handbook.* (Society of American Archivists, 1994). Online version by Stephen Miller. http://www.archivists.org/catalog/stds99/index.html.

Metadata

Baca, Murtha, ed. *Introduction to metadata: pathways to digital information.* (Getty Information Institute, 2002). Best introduction to metadata. http://www.getty.edu/research/conducting_research/standards/intrometadata.

Caplan, Priscilla. *Metadata fundamentals for all librarians.* (American Library Association, 2003).

EAD (Encoded Archival Description) Official Website. EAD documentation, standards, frequent updates and subscription to an online discussion group. http://www.loc.gov/ead.

METS (Metadata Encoding and Transmission Standard). http://www.loc.gov/standards/mets.

Using Dublin Core. Dublin Core Metadata Initiative, website maintained by Diane Hillmann. Frequently updated user guide. http://dublincore.org/documents/usageguide.

Controlled Vocabularies

AAT (Art & Architecture Thesaurus). http://www.getty.edu/research/conducting_research/vocabularies/aat.

ET (Ethnographic Thesaurus). In development at the time of this writing, but will be available on the American Folklore Society website, http://www.afsnet.org. The development group has a website, *Ethnographic thesaurus: a controlled vocabulary . . . ,* http://www.afsnet.org/thesaurus.

Library of Congress Authorities. Names and subjects. http://authorities.loc.gov.

MeSH (Medical Subject Headings). http://www.nlm.nih.gov/mesh.

TGN (Getty Thesaurus of Geographic Names). http://www.getty.edu/research/conducting_research/vocabularies/tgn.

PRESERVATION

AATA Online (Abstracts of international conservation literature), hosted by the Getty Research Institute. Free to registered users. http://aata.getty.edu/nps.

Blood, George. *Planning an audio preservation transfer project.* Presentation at the Society of American Archivists meeting, August 23, 2002, rev. January 12, 2005. http://www.safesoundarchive.com/PDF/AudioPreservProjectPlanning.pdf.

Bradley, Kevin, ed. *Guidelines on the production and preservation of digital audio objects.* Pub. no. IASA TC-04. (International Association of Sound and Audiovisual Archives, 2004). Order at http://www.iasa-web.org/iasa0075.htm.

Byers, Fred R. *Care and handling of CDs and DVDs: a guide for librarians and archivists.* (CLIR, 2003). http://www.clir.org/PUBS/reports/pub121/pub121.pdf

Casey, Mike, and Jon Dunn. *Audio preservation at Indiana University* (PowerPoint Presentation). www.dlib.indiana.edu/workshops/bbspring05slides/audio/casey.ppt.

Casey, Mike. "An overview of worldwide developments in digital preservation of audio," paper presented at the ARSC Conference, April 2, 2005. Available from the author, micasey@indiana.edu.

Dale, Robin, et al. *Audio preservation: a selective annotated bibliography and brief summary of current practices. (*American Library Association, 1998*).* http://www.ala.org/ala/alctscontent/alctspubsbucket/webpublications/alctspreservation/audiopreservatio/audiopres.pdf.

Digital Audio Best Practices. Version 2.5 (Collaborative Digitization Program, 2005). http://www.cdpheritage.org/digital/audio/documents/CDPDABP_1-2.pdf.

Fleischhauer, Carl. "Reformatting: a Library of Congress perspective." Paper delivered at the Preservation Conference: Digital Technology vs. Analog Technology, March 27, 2003. http://www.archives.gov/preservation/conferences/papers-2003/fleischauer.html.

Folk heritage collections in crisis. (CLIR, 2001). Based on a conference of the same name convened by the American Folklore Society and the American Folklife Center of the Library of Congress. http://www.clir.org/pubs/reports/pub96/contents.html.

Hess, Richard. *Restoration tips & notes: media formats & resources.* Audio preservationist provides tips for analog audio restoration, and blog on current topics. http://richardhess.com/notes/formats.

IASA Technical Committee. *The safeguarding of the audio heritage: ethics, principles and preservation strategy.* (IASA Technical Committee Papers, 2001). http://www.iasa-web.org/iasa0013.htm.

Kenney, Anne R., and Oya Rieger. *Moving theory into practice: digital imaging for libraries and archives. (RLG, 2000).* Handbook for digitizing cultural resources.

LOCKSS (Lots of Copies Keeps Stuff Safe). Open-source software for libraries and archives for preserving and providing access to digital collections. http://www.lockss.org.

Medina, Larry. "CDs, lies, and magnetic tapes." *Computer World* blog, posted January 10, 2006. http://www.computerworld.com/blogs/node/1552.

National Archives and Records Administration. *Long-term usability of optical media.* http://palimpsest.stanford.edu/bytopic/electronic-records/electronic-storage-media/critiss.html.

National Recording Preservation Board (Library of Congress). *Capturing analog sound for digital preservation: report of the roundtable discussion of best practices for transferring analog discs and tapes.* (Library of Congress, CLIR, 2006). http://www.clir.org/pubs/reports/pub137/pub137.pdf.

The NINCH guide to good practice in the digital representation and management of cultural heritage materials. (NINCH, 2002). http://www.nyu.edu/its/humanities/ninchguide.

Northeast Document Conservation Center. *Assessing preservation needs: a self-survey guide.* http://www.nedcc.org/selfsurvey/sec2b.htm.

Ogden, Sharon. *Preservation of library and archival materials: a manual.* 3rd ed. (Northeast Document Conservation Center, 1999). http://www.nedcc.org/plam3/manual.pdf.

Preservation Reformatting: Digital Technology vs. Analog Technology. (Preservation and Archives Professionals: 18th Annual Preservation Conference, 2003). http://www.archives.gov/preservation/conferences/2003. Includes papers by Howard Besser, Steven Puglia, Carl Fleischauer, and Ed Zwaneveld.

Smith, Abby, David Randal Allen, and Karen Allen. *Survey of the state of audio collections in academic libraries.* (CLIR, 2004). http://www.clir.org/pubs/reports/pub128/contents.html.

Sound directions: digital preservation and access for global audio heritage. (Indiana University Archives of Traditional Music and Harvard University's Archive of World Music). http://dlib.indiana.edu/projects/sounddirections.

The state of digital preservation: an international perspective. Conference proceedings: Documentation Abstracts, Inc. & Institutes for Information Science, April 24–25, 2002. (CLIR, 2002). http://www.clir.org/PUBS/reports/pub107/pub107.pdf.

Stuart, Lynn. *Preservation and access technology: a structured glossary of technical terms.* (CLIR, 1990). http://www.clir.org/pubs/abstract/pub10.html.

Sustainability of digital formats: planning for Library of Congress collections. http://www.digitalpreservation.gov/formats.

van Bogart, John W. C. *Magnetic tape storage and handling: a guide for libraries and archives.* (Commission on Preservation and Access: National Media Laboratory, 1995). http://www.clir.org/pubs/reports/pub54.

Websites for Preservation

ARSC (Association for Recorded Sound Collections). http://www.arsc-audio.org.

Collaborative Digitization Program (formerly Colorado Digitization Project). Tools and resources for digitizing historical materials. http://www.cdpheritage.org.

CoOl (Conservation online: resources for conservation professionals). Hosted by Stanford University. Portal for preservation and conservation. http://palimpsest.stanford.edu.

Historical voices. Tools for preserving and displaying cultural heritage. http://www.historicalvoices.org.

Image Permanence Institute. Hosted by Rochester Institute of Technology. http://www.imagepermanenceinstitute.org.

Library of Congress Preservation Portal. http://www.loc.gov/preserv.

National Digital Information and Infrastructure Program (NDIPP). Coordinates national strategy to collect, archive and preserve digital content. http://www.digitalpreservation.gov.

Washington State Library. *Digital Best Practices.* http://digitalwa.statelib.wa.gov/newsite/best.htm.

ORAL HISTORIES ON THE INTERNET

Arms, Caroline R. "Historical collections for the national digital library: lessons and challenges at the Library of Congress," *D-Lib* (April 1996). http://www.dlib.org/dlib/april96/loc/04c-arms.html.

Cohen, Daniel J., and Roy Rosenzweig. *Digital history: a guide to gathering, preserving and presenting the past on the Web.* (University of Pennsylvania Press, 2006). http://www.chnm.gmu.edu/digitalhistory. Also available in print.

A framework of guidance for building good digital collections. NISO Framework Advisory Group. 2nd ed. (National Information Standards Organization, 2004). http://www.niso.org/framework/Framework2.html.

NARA guidance for managing web records. (National Archives and Records Administration, 2005). http://www.archives.gov/records-mgmt/pdf/managing-web-records-index.pdf.

The NINCH guide to good practice in the digital representation and management of cultural heritage materials. (NINCH, 2002). http://www.nyu.edu/its/humanities/ninchguide.

"Oral History Online," media review by Michael Frisch, Jennifer Abraham, Jeff Suchanek, and Pamela Dean. *Oral history review* 32, 2 (Summer/Fall 2005). Reviews the Alexander Street

Press database *Oral History Online.* (http://www.alexanderstreet.com/products/orhi.htm)

Save Our Sounds. http://www.saveoursounds.org.

Schneider, William. *So they understand: cultural issues in oral history.* (Utah State University Press, 2002). Ethical issues concerning oral histories on the Internet.

Sound directions: digital preservation and access for global audio heritage. (Indiana University Archives of Traditional Music and Harvard University's Archive of World Music). http://dlib.indiana.edu/projects/sounddirections.

SURVEYS & STUDIES RELATING TO ORAL HISTORIES IN ARCHIVES

Brewster, Karen. *Internet access to oral recordings: finding the issues.* (Oral History Program, University of Alaska, Fairbanks, 2000). Ethical issues of posting oral histories on the World Wide Web. http://www.uaf.edu/library/oralhistory/brewster1/index.html

Mackay, Nancy. *Curating oral histories: survey results.* Survey upon which this book is based, concerned with the state of oral histories in archives. http://www.nancymackay.net/curating/finalSurveyResults.htm.

A public trust at risk: the heritage health index report on the state of America's collections. (Heritage Preservation with the Institute of Museum and Library Services, 2005). http://www.heritagepreservation.org/HHI/

Smith, Abby, David Randal Allen, and Karen Allen. *Survey of the state of audio collections in academic libraries.* (CLIR, 2004). http://www.clir.org/pubs/reports/pub128/pub128.pdf

Survey of folk heritage collections: summary of results. American Folklore Society, American Folklife Center of the Library of Congress, and the Society for Ethnomusicology. (CLIR, 2000). http://www.clir.org/pubs/reports/pub96/appendix2.html

Walch, Virginia Irons. *Where history begins: a report on historical records repositories in the United States.* (Council of State Historical Records Coordinators, 1998). http://www.statearchivists.org/reports/HRRS/HRRSALL.PDF

Zorich, Diane. *A survey of Digital Cultural Heritage Initiatives (DCHIs) and their sustainability concerns.* (CLIR, 2003). http://www.clir.org/pubs/abstract/pub118abst.html.

ONLINE PROJECT GUIDES

Capturing the living past: an oral history primer. (Developed by Barbara Sommer and Mary Kay Quinlan for the Nebraska State Historical Society, 2005). http://www.nebraskahistory.org/lib-arch/research/audiovis/oral_history.

Conducting oral histories. California Council for the Humanities. http://www.calhum.org/Resources/oralHistories.htm.

Handbook for oral history in the National Park Service (Draft). 2005. http://www.cr.nps.gov/history/oh/oral.htm.

Oral history techniques: how to organize and conduct oral history interviews. (Barbara Truesdell, Indiana University Center for the Study of History and Memory). http://www.indiana.edu/~cshm/techniques.html

SOHP how to guide. Southern Oral History Program (University of North Carolina). http://www.sohp.org/howto/guide/index.html.

StoryCorps. http://storycorps.net.

Sunnyvale voices: from settlers to Silicon, project design manual, by Steve Sloan and Tony Calvo. (Sunnyvale Public Library, 2000). Comprehensive project manual, including budgets, staff needs and lessons learned. http://sunnyvale.ca.gov/voices/Manual.pdf

ORGANIZATIONS AND PROFESSIONAL ASSOCIATIONS

In a field as rapidly evolving as ours, the best way to get current information is to go straight to the source. These associations and organizations will keep you up to date with workshops, publications, online discussion groups, and practical tips. This section is reproduced online and will be updated periodically at http://www.nancymackay.net/curating/networking.htm.

Alaska Native Knowledge Network, http://www.ankn.uaf.edu. Sponsored by the University of Alaska, Fairbanks. Portal for exchanging information related to Alaskan native knowledge systems and broader cultural issues.
• Publications • Online Resources (Curriculum) • Professional standards (Guidelines for respecting cultural knowledge. Adopted 2000)

American Association of Museums (AAM), http://www.aam-us.org/
• Conference • Publications • Professional standards (AAM Accreditation Program)

American Association for State and Local History (AASLH), http://www.aaslh.org.
• Conference • Publications: *History news*, technical leaflets • Online Resources • Professional standards (*Statement of Professional Standards and Ethics*, 2002) • Workshops

American Folklore Society (AFS), http://afsnet.org.
• Conference • Publications: *Journal of American Folklore, AFS News*

American Historical Association (AHA), http://www.historians.org.
• Conference • Online resources for graduate students, history teachers, and public historians • Publications: *American Historical Review*, publication series • Professional standards (*Statement on standards of professional conduct*, Rev. 2005).

American Library Association (ALA), http://www.ala.org.
• Conference • Online discussion groups for many special interest groups • Publications: *American Libraries*, large publication list of books and pamphlets for library professionals • Professional standards: *Library Bill of Rights*, links to standards and guidelines for library specialties. • This large organization has many special interest groups and regional affiliates.

American Society for Information Science and Technology (ASIS), http://www.asis.org.
• Conference • Online discussion group: series of special interest discussion groups sponsored by ASIS • Publications: *Annual Review of Information Science and Technology, Journal of the American Society for Information Science and Technology, ASIS&T Bulletin* annual conference proceedings • This large organization has a number of special interest groups.

ARMA International (previously Association of Records Managers and Administrators), http://www.arma.org.
• Conference • Publications: *Journal of Information Management*, pamphlet series • Online resources: online courses and seminars

Association for Recorded Sound Collections (ARSC), http://www.arsc-audio.org.
• Conference • Online discussion group • Publications: *ARSC Journal, ARSC Newsletter, ARSC Bulletin,* conference proceedings are available on CD.

Association of Moving Image Archivists (AMIA), http://www.amianet.org.
• Conference • Online discussion group • Publications: *The Moving Image, AMIA Newsletter* • Online resources

Association of Personal Historians (APH), http://www.personalhistorians.org. Devoted to collecting life histories of individuals and families.
• Conference • Online resources • Regional chapters

Center for Digital Storytelling, http://www.storycenter.org. A nonprofit organization devoted to using digital technology for telling stories.
• Online resources • Workshops & tutorials

Center for History and New Media (CHNM), http://chnm.gmu.edu. Sponsored by George Mason University, the Center supports projects which use digital technology to bring history to a wide audience.
• Online resources: free digital tools (such as a survey builder and timeline builder)

Center for Internet and Society, (CIS), http://cyberlaw.stanford.edu/index.shtml. Sponsored by Stanford University Law School, the CIS offers cutting edge thinking on legal and ethical issues in the Internet Age.
• Conference • Special interest blogs, RSS available • Newsletter

Council of State Archivists (COSA), http://www.statearchivists.org.
• Conference • Publications • Online resources • Workshops & tutorials

Council on Library and Information Resources (CLIR), http://www.clir.org. Independent, nonprofit organization devoted to increasing public access to information in all formats through research, publications and educational programs.
• Publications: scholarly reports on information technology issues. Publications available online • Workshops & institutes

Conservation online (CoOL), http://palimpsest.stanford.edu. Web portal for conservation and preservation, hosted by Stanford University. Frequently updated.
• Online resources • Professional standards

Creative Commons, http://creativecommons.org. Nonprofit organization offering a flexible copyright option for creative work. This is an option that lies between full copyright and public domain.
• Online discussion group • Online resources

Getty Research Institute, http://www.getty.edu/research. Sponsors initiatives on digitization and metadata for cultural objects.
• Online discussion group • Publications • Online resources • Workshops & tutorials

H-NET (Humanities and Social Sciences Online), http://www.h-net.org. Network of scholars and teachers who use the web to distribute information to a wide audience.
• Online discussion groups: supports a large number of moderated discussion groups in particular topics in the sciences and humanities, including H-ORALHIST (oral history), H-MUSEUM (museum studies) and H-PUBLIC (public history) • Publications: online book reviews.

Heritage Preservation, http://www.heritagepreservation.org. Nonprofit organization dedicated to preserving cultural heritage.
• Publications: large catalog of print and online reports and curriculum materials, including *Heritage Health Index*, a comprehensive survey to assess the condition and preservation needs of the institution's historical collections in the United States.

Image Permanence Institute, http://www.imagepermanenceinstitute.org. Hosted by College of Imaging Arts and Sciences, Rochester Institute of Technology. Devoted to scientific research in the preservation of recorded information.
• Publications • Workshops

Independent Media Arts Preservation (IMAP), http://www.imappreserve.org. Nonprofit service, education, and advocacy organization committed to the preservation of noncommercial electronic media.
• Online resources • Workshops & tutorials

Institute of Museum and Library Services, http://www.imls.gov. Independent federal grant making agency which administers Library Services and Technology Act (LSTA) grants to libraries and museums. The website serves as a portal for resources useful to libraries and museums.
• Conferences • Publications: *Primary source newsletter*, others available online and in print • Online resources • Workshops & tutorials

International Association of Sound and Audiovisual Archives (IASA), http://www.iasaweb.org.
• Conference • Publications: *IASA Journal*, guidelines and best practices for cataloging sound recordings, preservation of digital audio and others • Online resources • Professional standards

International Council on Archives (ICA), http://www.ica.org. International association devoted to preservation and use of archives. Regional chapters and special interest groups.
• Conference • Online discussion group • Publications • Online resources • Workshops & tutorials • Professional standards

International Federation of Library Associations and Institutions (IFLA), http://www.ifla.org.
• Conference • Online discussion group: sponsors 50 special interest online discussion groups • Publications: *IFLA Journal, International Cataloging and Bibliographic Control Journal*, numerous reports, conference proceedings, newsletters and best practices • Online resources • Professional standards

International Oral History Association (IOHA), http://www.ioha.fgv.br.
• Conference • Online discussion group • Publications: *Words and silences* (journal), *IOHA Newsletter*

International Organization for Standardization (ISO), http://www.iso.org. An international, nongovernmental organization devoted to establishing and enforcing standards.
• Online discussion group: e-mail newsletter • Publications • Online resources • Professional standards

Library of Congress, http://www.loc.gov. Serves as a portal for the Library of Congress catalog, American Memory Project, Veterans Oral History Project, and information on digital preservation.
• Publications • Online resources • Workshops & tutorials • Professional standards

MATRIX, The Center for Humane Arts, Letters and Social Sciences Online, http://matrix.msu.edu. Sponsored by Michigan State University, this center supports the use of digital technology for projects in the humanities and social sciences. *Historical Voices*, serves as a model for best practices for a digital repository.
• Online resources • Best practices

National Archives and Records Administration (NARA), http://www.archives.gov. Portal to areas of interest to archivists and records managers.
• Conference • Publications • Online resources • Workshops: Modern Archives Institute • Professional standards

National Council on Public History (NCPH), http://www.ncph.org.

• Conference • Online discussion group: H-PUBLIC • Publications: *Public historian, Public history news*, and other pamphlets and videos.

National Initiative for a Networked Cultural Heritage (NINCH), http://www.ninch.org. This nonprofit coalition of arts, humanities, and social science organizations created to assure leadership into a digital environment.
• Online discussion groups • Publications • Best practices • Workshops

Northeast Document Conservation Center (NEDCC), http://www.nedcc.org. Nonprofit organization devoted to the conservation of paper artifacts.
• Conference • Publications available online • Online resources • Workshops & tutorials

OCLC (Online Computer Library Center), http://www.oclc.org. A nonprofit computer library and research organization, best known for WorldCat, its international union catalog, available to the public in most libraries. Announced merger with RLG in Spring 2006.
• Online discussion group: various lists based on special interests • Publications • Online resources • Institutes, workshops, webcasts, and individual consulting • Professional standards for bibliographic description

Online AudioVisual Catalogers (OLAC), http://ublib.buffalo.edu/libraries/units/cts/olac.
• Conference • Online discussion group • Publications • Online resources

Oral History Association (OHA), http://omega.dickinson.edu/organizations/oha.
• Conference • Online discussion group: H-ORALHIST • Publications: *Oral history review, OHA Newsletter*, pamphlet series including *Oral history & the law* • Online resources

• Professional standards: *Evaluation guidelines*, Rev. 2000. Check also state and regional associations.

Organization of American Historians (OAH), http://www.oah.org.
• Conference • Publications: *Journal of American History, OAH Newsletter*, curriculum resources, and others. Also has regional affiliates.

Program for Cooperative Cataloging (PCC), http://www.loc.gov/catdir/pcc. International committee designed to expand access to library collections by providing useful, timely, and cost-effective cataloging that meets internationally accepted standards.
• Committee meeting at ALA conference • Online resources • Professional standards

Research Libraries Group (RLG), http://www.rlg.org. International nonprofit organization that supports bibliographic and preservation services to cultural institutions. Announced merger with OCLC in Spring 2006.
• Conference • Online discussion group: many discussion groups on specific topics • Publications • Online resources • Best practices

Society of American Archivists (SAA), http://www.archivists.org.
• Conference • Online discussion group • Publications: *American Archivist*, books and pamphlets • Online resources • Workshops & tutorials • Professional standards: *Code of ethics for archivists*. Rev. 2005. Check also state and regional societies.

United States Copyright Office. http://www.copyright.gov. Administers the registration and regulation of copyright in the United States.
• Publications • Online resources

INDEX

ABOUT THE AUTHOR

Photo by Jonathan Ryshpan

Nancy MacKay has been straddling the line between libraries and oral history for almost twenty years. As a librarian she has worked with special collections, cataloging, and music in various academic settings. She discovered oral history accidentally, by picking up a flyer for a free oral history workshop offered by the LEGACY project, and has been hooked ever since. As an oral historian she has conducted oral history projects, taught oral history workshops, advised student projects, and consulted on community projects. She currently combines these fields at Mills College, as Head of Library Technical Services and coordinator for the Oakland Living History Program. She lives in the San Francisco Bay Area. See more at http://www.nancy mackay.net/